The CHALLENGE of DEVELOPMENT in LATIN AMERICA

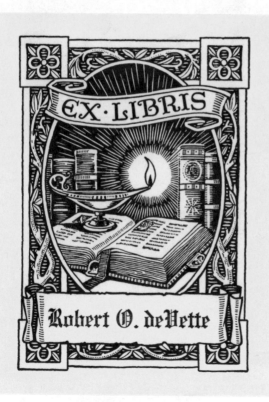

The CHALLENGE of DEVELOPMENT in LATIN AMERICA

VICTOR L. URQUIDI

Translated from the Spanish by
Marjory M. Urquidi

Foreword by
Frank Tannenbaum

FREDERICK A. PRAEGER, *Publisher*
New York • London

FREDERICK A. PRAEGER, *Publisher*
111 Fourth Ave., New York 3, N.Y., U.S.A.
77-79 Charlotte Street, London W.1, England

Published in the United States of America in 1964
by Frederick A. Praeger, Inc., Publisher

First published in Mexico in 1962 under the title
VIABILIDAD ECONÓMICA DE AMÉRICA LATINA
by Fondo de Cultura Económica

Library of Congress Catalog Card Number: 64–16692

Printed in the United States of America

Foreword

In *The Challenge of Development in Latin America,* Víctor
Urquidi has written a book that deserves wide and careful reading by all those who are even remotely concerned with our relations with underdeveloped countries in general and with Latin
America in particular. What Mr. Urquidi has to say is important
not only because of the subjects he deals with and the manner in
which he treats them, but for the authority with which he speaks.
An economist trained in England, he has worked with and for
the United Nations Economic Commission for Latin America,
has played a leading role in developing the Central American
Common Market Organization, and has represented the Mexican
Government in a great many of its international economic negotiations. Among his many roles, he served, for about fifteen years,
as the editor of *El Trimestre Económico,* undoubtedly the most
important economic journal published in Latin America; and he
is now, and has been for years, a close adviser of the Mexican
Secretary of the Treasury. Clearly, whatever Mr. Urquidi has to
say about economic development and about American policies
on development, whether private or governmental, will be widely
noted in Latin America and ought to be read with care in this
country as well. For, in some degree, he speaks, without pretend-
ing to, for an entire generation of Latin American economists
and policy makers.

Since what Mr. Urquidi has to say will be highly unpalatable
to many Americans, and may even seem wrong, it is important

to emphasize that Mr. Urquidi is a friend and admirer of the United States, that he is basically a pragmatist, and, as the reader will note, a realist in the best sense of the word. Few economists are as aware as he is of the handicaps, shortcomings, and inadequacies in the economic, political, and social pattern as it now exists in Latin America. Mr. Urquidi is also aware— and in the modern world this is an uncommon virtue—that there are "no perfect solutions." He knows from history and from his own experience how recalcitrant and refractory the political and cultural environment can be and how self-defeating the best projects may prove.

Yet in this book he makes a sober attempt to face the economic difficulties that confront Latin America and to prescribe some tentative solutions for them. That the solutions will seem extremely nationalistic must be put down to the fact that the economist looking out upon an industrialized society from any underdeveloped part of the world, including Latin America, seems to have no other ground to stand upon. The English and American experiences seem to him not to fit the special economic needs of a raw-material–producing country facing the highly dynamic industrial society it has to deal and compete with. The very catalogue of issues that dominate discussions of economic development are different from those that, say, an American economist would deal with if he were writing about the rate of growth of the American economy. The fact is that the Latin American is really writing about *political* economy, that is, about the total state of affairs—about the nation in its relation to other nations, about the state's role in the efforts to stimulate a rate of growth sufficiently large to keep up with the expanding population, about the relation of education to economic development, about honesty in government, about the amount of, and the conditions under which, foreign capital is politically acceptable, about the conditions of technical and scientific development, and about the relations of the government to all these and to many other things besides. If Mr. Urquidi seems unduly committed to government intervention, the reasons are clear: He writes within the Spanish tradition of centralization; he believes economic development is so urgent a matter that it must involve immediate public policy; and, finally, he sees no alternatives in a small and insufficiently experienced middle class incapable of getting on with the task of national economic development.

Mr. Urquidi belongs to the generation of economists who believe in economic planning, but he has the virtue of recognizing its limits, for he opposes centralized administration and argues that localities and regions ought to administer their own development within the large scheme. He also favors private investment and private business that contribute to economic development, and he considers the Alliance for Progress to be the "only road open to Latin America that guarantees us democracy, liberty, and personal dignity."

This is a book on the political economy of Latin America in the mid-twentieth century—and because it is that, it deserves careful reading, especially by those who will most disagree with it.

FRANK TANNENBAUM

Columbia University
New York, N.Y.
March, 1964

Preface

MY PURPOSE is to examine the over-all condition and prospects of the Latin American economy. There is a strong temptation to go beyond this subject and enter into more general observations. However, discussions of Latin America so frequently disregard the economic elements that I feel it worthwhile to single out and define them, and let other specialists deal elsewhere with the broader aspects. It is not easy to isolate the economic factors. In fact, it would be a mistake to ignore the social and political setting in which the problems of the Latin American economy evolve. Many economic problems can be explained only in terms of the political and social situation, and I therefore refer to these conditions as the occasion requires.

I have entitled my book *The Challenge of Development in Latin America,* conscious of the fact that there is no simple solution to our problems, but confident that Latin America will respond to the challenge. I endeavor to show that in Latin America —unlike central Africa and certain countries of Southeast Asia— there exist more positive than negative factors. Nevertheless, in order to emphasize the achievements, it is occasionally necessary to call attention to the many powerful forces working against progress, which can and must be defeated.

Latin America is undergoing considerable changes in the structure of its economy, but one often hears or reads the commonplaces of twenty or thirty years ago about its agriculture and industry, its resources, its relations with world markets and sources of capital, its monetary and financial affairs, the extent of government intervention in the private sector, etc. It is thus essential to establish some basic facts about the Latin American economy today and to analyze trends in the world economy that affect, or may later affect, Latin America's evolution. Against this background rests much of the subsequent discussion of inflation, the role of foreign capital, the social and institutional conditions of development, economic integration, and programming. The Alliance for Progress derives directly from past failures to harmonize this complex set of economic, social, and institutional relationships in a way that would ensure a sufficiently high rate of development. Because of its essential importance, I devote some space to tracing the events and examining the main ideas that led to the signing of the Charter of Punta del Este in 1961.

Aware that much more can be said than what I have tried to express concisely in this book, I trust to the reader's indulgence and only hope that he will share my concern with exploring the problems of Latin America.

This is a translation of a series of lectures I gave at El Colegio Nacional, Mexico City, in October, 1961. Revised and expanded, and with a statistical appendix, they appeared in book form in 1962, under the title *Viabilidad Económica de América Latina* (México, Fondo de Cultura Económica). I have not attempted to bring the statistical tables up to date, partly because this book is an account of the Latin American economy as it was prior to the Alliance for Progress, and also because the incomplete information at present available on events in 1962–63 does not alter significantly the picture and the trends encompassed in an analysis running through 1960–61, despite incipient progress under the new policies implied in the Alliance.

V. L. U.

Tlacopac, D.F.
December, 1963

Contents

APPENDIX TABLES

1. Some Structural Problems

DESPITE A GROWING tendency to the contrary, it is advisable to consider the twenty republics of Latin America as a single region. The vast differences within this region make it easy to argue that a particular statement is not valid because it does not apply to one or another of the republics. However, the dissimilarities between various sections of a country do not prevent their sharing traits, trends, and events representative of the entire nation. In the same way, there exist in Latin America circumstances and characteristics typical of the region as a whole. It is distracting and even misleading always to point out the exceptions, especially when they are advantageous or relate to one's own country. The predominant feature, whether favorable or not, is the characteristic one and usually the one that commands the most attention.

Latin America needs to accept the concept of *a* Latin America and *a* Latin American economy, not several, if it wishes to succeed in its search for solutions that will assure the progress of all the region. The foregoing observations are even more relevant to its position vis-à-vis the rest of the world. Latin American solidarity in economics, as in other areas, must be unqualified.

Nevertheless, when the situation is examined as a whole, a definition of its components affords better perspective and focuses attention on what is significant.

Latin America's striking rate of population growth, the highest in the world, is a primary factor of its economy. The total population of Latin America, which by the middle of 1962 reached almost 210 million, or 5 million more than the United States and Canada together and almost as many as the Soviet Union, is expected to increase by about 2.6 per cent per annum.[1] (See Table 1.) At this rate of growth, the population of Latin America will increase by 85 per cent in twenty-five years. By 1980, there will be some 333 million Latin Americans. As long as the death rate continues to decline and the proportion of population in the lower age groups continues to rise, any slight drop in the birth rate due to urbanization will hardly affect the over-all rate of increment, and population growth is not likely to slacken. The anticipated annual 2.6 per cent rate of increase in Latin America's population may be compared with the 1.7 per cent per annum used in projections for the United States economy[2] and the 0.6 per cent in projections for the Western European economy.[3] It is assumed that the population of central Africa will increase by 1.4 per cent per annum.[4] At these rates, Latin America's population will double in only 27 years, whereas Western Europe's will need 115 years, central Africa's 50 years, and the United States' 41 years.

Some of the consequences of Latin America's high rate of population growth, which in many cases are unfavorable to economic development, will be discussed later on. It is interesting to note that in 1962 the two most populous countries, Brazil and Mexico, together contained half the inhabitants of Latin America: 69 million Brazilians and 37 million Mexicans.

[1] Population and other data are based on information published by the Economic Commission for Latin America (ECLA), *Economic Bulletin for Latin America*, V (November, 1960), Statistical Supplement, and on other sources cited in the Statistical Appendix to this book.

[2] National Planning Association, *Long-Range Projections for Economic Growth: the American Economy in 1970*, Table 2.

[3] United Nations, *The Future Growth of World Population*, Appendix C, derived from Table I (A).

[4] UNESCO/Economic Commission for Africa, *Conference of African States on the Development of Education in Africa, Final Report* (Addis Ababa, May 15–25, 1961). Derived from Chap. IV, Table I.

Brazilians alone represented 33 per cent of the total. These two nationalities were followed by 22 million Argentines, 15½ million Colombians, 11½ million Peruvians, and 11½ million Central Americans (excluding Panama). The rest of Latin America comprised barely a fifth of the total number of inhabitants. (See Table 1.)

Since the numerical preponderance of Brazilians and Mexicans is accompanied by some of the highest birth rates and by death rates that are, if not the lowest, at least average, the population growth rate of these two countries combined—about 3.0 per cent per annum—exceeds the population growth rate of Latin America as a whole. Mexicans and Brazilians will thus account for progressively higher proportions of the total Latin American population, at the expense of nationalities with lower growth rates, such as the Argentines, Uruguayans, Chileans, and Cubans. At present rates, the combined Mexican and Brazilian populations will reach almost 172 million in 1980 (63 million and 109 million, respectively), or 52 per cent of the total number of Latin Americans. If these rates are sustained, by the year 2000 those two nations will constitute more than 53 per cent of the total: 297 million out of 556 million. Although Costa Rica, the Dominican Republic, Guatemala, and Nicaragua increase their populations by more than 3 per cent per annum, and Colombia, Peru, and Venezuela approach that rate, they will not change the demographic pattern established by Brazil and Mexico.

Broadly speaking, the Latin American population is young: in 1960, slightly more than 40 per cent were less than fifteen years old, following a reduction in the mortality of infants and children under five. In this respect, there is great uniformity. Only Argentina and Uruguay are like the United States and Canada in having young people make up less than 33 per cent of the population, the smaller percentage resulting partly from immigration and also partly from a low adult death rate. In Brazil and Mexico, the proportion of young people is higher than average for Latin America, and in some of the less populated countries it is very nearly 45 per cent. (See Table 2.)

It is estimated that about 54 per cent of Latin Americans live in rural areas. Mexico and Brazil, with roughly this distribution, bear out the thesis that the percentage of rural population is an index to a country's degree of economic development, since they have attained an intermediate level that is characteristic of Latin American life. Mexico is somewhat more urbanized than Brazil: 51 per cent of its population is urban, as against the latter's 37 per cent. Definitions of rural population differ, but it is significant that in 1960 fourteen Latin American countries were classified as having a rural population of 50 per cent or more, with Honduras and Haiti as high as 75 and 83 per cent. Five countries —Uruguay, Argentina, Chile, Venezuela, and Cuba—ranged from 19 to 45 per cent. The large proportions of rural population in Latin American countries contrast with about 30 per cent in the United States and Canada, and 44 per cent in France.

The occupational structure also reveals significant features. The substantial rural population suggests that most of the economically active population of Latin America are engaged in agriculture and livestock raising; actual estimates are that slightly more than 50 per cent are so employed, a percentage close to that for the rural population. In 1950, manufacturing absorbed less than 15 per cent of the total labor force, mining a little more than 1 per cent, and construction not quite 4 per cent. But services, including transportation, distribution, banking and other facilities, and government, employed 25 per cent of the economically active population. (See Table 4.) More recent figures are unavailable; the great Census of the Americas of 1960, despite its electronic brains, still has not delivered its results. It is probable that agricultural employment has dropped to 50 per cent and the manufacturing labor force has increased to 16 per cent. (See Table 7.) But the fact remains that in spite of industrialization, Latin America utilizes more of its population in agriculture and associated activities than in any other branch of economic employment.

More Latin Americans are engaged in farming than in manufacturing or services.

Only a few countries are exceptions. In two, Argentina and Uruguay, the proportion of manufacturing workers is higher than 20 per cent; in three, these plus Chile, less than 40 per cent —actually, in these cases, less than 30 per cent—of the population are occupied in agriculture. (See Table 4.)

Although women today are better educated and enjoy increasing opportunities for employment in services, the female sector of the labor force is still small, perhaps no more than 15 or 18 per cent of the total. However, women represent a very important labor reserve.

In general, the considerable proportion of the population employed in commercial and distributing activities is a potential source of manpower for industrial activities that may develop in the future.

As a rule, the percentage of the population that is gainfully employed is lower in Latin America—30 to 40 per cent—than in Europe and the United States, where it ranges from 40 to 50 per cent. For the female population alone, the percentage is markedly lower.

The average living standard of the Latin American people is not very high, no matter what qualifications are attached to the significance of estimated figures and comparisons involving them. The gross product per person in 1961 can be calculated as equivalent to about $320 at 1950 prices, or about $371 at 1960 prices. In 1960, it was $366, or not quite one-eighth that of the United States, between one-sixth and one-fifth that of Canada, somewhat less than one-third that of Western Europe, possibly a little more than one-half that of the Soviet Union and Puerto Rico, and roughly equal to that of Japan. (See Table 5.) But Latin America's product per person of $366 was three and a half to four times that of central Africa and almost five times that of underdeveloped Asia. Nevertheless, Latin America has a low per capita product and a low living standard, if these concepts are considered analogous; little comfort can be derived from comparison with central Africa or Southeast Asia.

Regional averages mask striking differences between the component countries. In Europe, Portugal, Spain, and Greece have a per capita product that barely matches that of Latin America, but France, Germany, Great Britain, and Sweden boast a per capita product three to four times that of Latin America. In Asia, Indonesia has a per capita product calculated at barely $65, and in India it is about $70. In Africa, Ghana has a per capita product two-thirds that of Latin America; in well-populated countries, such as the Congo, Nigeria, and Sudan, it certainly is less than $100 per person.

Similarly, a considerable variation is found within Latin America. In only Argentina, Venezuela, and Costa Rica, which have 15 per cent of the total Latin American population, is the product per person more than $400. Two-thirds of the population of Latin America inhabit Brazil, Mexico, Colombia, Uruguay, Chile, Panama, and Cuba, and have a per capita product of between $300 and $400. In Ecuador, Peru, the rest of Central America, Paraguay, and the Dominican Republic, it is between $100 and $300, with an average of possibly $150 to $200. In Bolivia and Haiti, it is estimated to be no more than about $100.

It would appear, then, that the 1960 average of $366 is fairly representative of all Latin America. In just two countries, Argentina and Uruguay, does the living standard approach even half that of the most advanced countries of Europe (in Venezuela's case the national and not the domestic product should be taken for this purpose). The living standard in two countries, Bolivia and Haiti, is hardly any higher than that in India and Sudan. In Colombia, Chile, Mexico, and Brazil, the living standard is just under the Latin American average. Again, Brazil and Mexico may be considered typical.

National averages cannot be evaluated without taking into account the important internal differences that they conceal. In the United States, for example, the states' per capita incomes vary by up to 150 per cent, with the lowest in Mississippi and the highest in Delaware. In Brazil, the third of the population living in the Northeast has an average income of $100, not much more than that of Bolivians, while the third living in the main industrial and coffee-growing areas enjoys an average income almost on a par with that of Argentines. In Mexico, the per capita product of the wealthy states is 10 to 12 times that of the poor states.[5]

In Latin America, such discrepancies, which result from uneven rates of development and disparate resources, climates, populations, and social institutions, do not have to be so extreme either within or between countries. Without question, an essential element of future economic development in Latin America must be a collective effort to raise rapidly the level of productivity of its most backward countries and areas.

Significantly, 87 per cent of the gross domestic product of Latin America originates in just seven countries: 30 per cent in Brazil and 18 per cent in Argentina, which together account for almost one-half, and 15 per cent in Mexico, 11 per cent in Venezuela, 7 per cent in Colombia, 4 per cent in Chile, and 2 per cent in Peru. (See Table 6.) These seven countries contain 81 per cent of the population. The thirteen remaining countries contribute only 13 per cent of the product and have 19 per cent of the population. Consequently, what happens to the economies of the first seven countries largely determines the condition and trend of the Latin American economy. It is, therefore, important to be familiar with their structural aspects, especially those of Brazil, Argentina, and Mexico, in order to interpret shifts in the Latin American economy. A bad crop year in Argentina, a slack in the industrial development of Brazil or Mexico, a strike in the mines of Chile or the oil fields of Venezuela, a drop in the price of Colombian

[5] P. Lamartine Yates, *El desarrollo regional de México* (México, Banco de México, 1961), Tables 14 and 15. The estimates given in this study may exaggerate the differences, but in no case would the latter be less than 5 to 7 times.

or Brazilian coffee—any of these can have a serious impact on the Latin American economy. Similarly, favorable events may have a beneficial effect. Long-term trends are also dependent on the development of these countries. The recent industrialization of Latin America was spurred by the relatively rapid industrial growth of Mexico and Brazil, and the progress of agriculture has been severely hampered by its stagnation in Argentina, Brazil, and Chile.

Bearing in mind the pre-eminence of the above seven countries, Latin America's total gross product may be broken down into the following components: manufacturing, 24 per cent; agriculture and livestock raising, 20 per cent; mining and petroleum, 6 per cent; construction, 3 per cent; and transportation, commercial, financial, governmental, and other services, the remaining 47 per cent. (See Table 7.) Correlating these figures with the distribution of the gainfully employed shows that the activity that is least productive per capita is agriculture and livestock raising: it employs 50 per cent of the working population to generate 20 per cent of the product. Construction, not a very productive activity, has a per capita output nearly twice that of agriculture and livestock raising. Manufacturing output per person is 3.8 times that of agriculture; and mining and petroleum yield a per capita product 15 times that of agriculture and livestock raising, and 4 times that of manufacturing. (See Table 7.) These rough figures show that agriculture, which supports more than half the population of Latin America, is unproductive in comparison with other activities—a statement that applies more to countries like Brazil and Mexico than to others. Here is an indication that, irrespective of over-all and per-worker gains in industrial output, an effort must be made to narrow the gap between the productivity of agriculture and that of other activities. An upsurge in the former would have a favorable effect on the total gross product of Latin America and would make possible a substantial rise in the living standard of a majority of its inhabitants.

The facts presented so far may serve as background for an examination of recent economic development. From 1951 to 1960, the average annual growth rate of Latin America's gross product was 4.5 per cent. (See Table 8.) A comparison with the annual population growth of 2.5 per cent shows that the per capita product went up, on the average, by 1.95 per cent per annum. But, although the increase in product per person was 2.1 per cent per annum from 1951 to 1955, it declined to 1.7 per cent from 1956 to 1960. This slowing down of development was largely the result of a lagging agriculture. While the latter raised its production by only 42 per cent during the 1951–60 period, manufacturing raised its output by 97 per cent, at an average annual rate of 7 per cent, in contrast to agriculture's 3.6 per cent. During the 1951–55 period, there was less spread between manufacturing, which expanded by 30 per cent, and agriculture, which expanded by 22 per cent. But during the 1956–60 period, the increase in industrial output accelerated to 52 per cent, while the gain in agricultural production slumped to only 16 per cent. In view of the large proportion of economically active people engaged in agriculture and the latter's low productivity, the lack of agricultural growth is an extremely serious problem. From 1951 to 1960, the per capita product of agriculture barely rose by 11 per cent, or 1.1 per cent per annum. On the other hand, industrial output per person rose by 54 per cent, or 4.4 per cent per annum. Both agriculture's pattern of slow growth and industry's pattern of relatively rapid growth need to be analyzed further.

Latin American agriculture has fallen behind most in livestock raising, which between 1950 and 1959 increased by only 15 per cent, or less than the population. Meanwhile, crop output rose by 45 per cent. (See Table 9.) An examination of the 1958 figure, 39 per cent greater than that for 1950, reveals that wheat, sugar, rice, and cacao were among the products that expanded most slowly (wheat weighs heavily in the total). Corn (maize), coffee, and cotton had a brisker, although not very high, growth rate. (See Table 10.)

Wheat production in Latin America in 1958 was barely 24 per cent above that for 1950. Argentina, which produces 60 per cent of Latin American wheat, showed practically no increase, even taking into account the annual fluctuations. But Mexico doubled its output, and Chile raised its volume by 50 per cent. Although their combined production is only one-fourth of the total, they account for most of the 1951–58 general increment. Latin America's peak year in wheat was 1955, thanks to a fairly good crop in Argentina.

Corn (maize) production increased only 31 per cent from 1951 to 1958 (excluding the abnormal year 1950), which may be partly explained by the stagnation in Argentine production, normally about one-fifth of the total, and the meager growth of Brazilian production, now more than one-third. Mexico, today Latin America's second-ranking corn-producing country, has raised its output by almost one-half since 1951, which has largely offset the poor progress made in other countries. Latin America's corn crop falls far short of its requirements.

Almost all the increment in sugar production was achieved by Brazil and Mexico until 1958. That year, both countries reached twice their 1950 volume, and their combined share of the total came to 30 per cent. But Cuba's output, which ordinarily constitutes one-half to two-thirds of Latin America's sugar production, remained stationary, save for an exceptional crop in 1952.

Cotton production in Latin America has increased less than is commonly assumed. Although Mexico doubled its output between 1950 and 1958 (this last being an outstanding year), Brazil's crop, which still accounts for 28 per cent of the total, has been at a standstill for some time. Because Mexico represents nearly 40 per cent of the total, over-all cotton production increased by almost 50 per cent during the 1950–58 period. Most of this expansion had taken place by 1955.

Latin America's coffee production also rose by 50 per cent. Brazil, which produces 50 to 60 per cent of the total, managed to increase its output by more than two-thirds. But Colombia, another large producer (20 to 25 per cent of the total), raised its output by less than 40 per cent. There is no reason to believe that Latin America's coffee production has been insufficient.

The two principal banana-producing countries—not Central American, as is generally assumed—are Brazil and Ecuador; they have been responsible for almost the entire increment of 35 per cent in this crop between 1950 and 1958.

These data on Latin America's leading products confirm the fact that agriculture has progressed slowly, especially in cereals, and that livestock raising has advanced even less speedily.

In contrast to agriculture, the 1951–60 development of industry—even within a moderate growth of only 4.5 per cent in the aggregate gross product—has been striking. Steel production in Latin America in 1960 has exceeded 4.5 million tons, more than three times the 1950 output; cement, paper, and paperboard have more than doubled; petroleum and its derivatives and chemical products have increased by at least 130 per cent. Most of the increase in Latin American industrial production can be attributed to Brazil, Mexico, and Argentina, followed by Chile and Colombia. Not all the manufacturing sectors have taken such strides forward. In particular, the textile industry, despite its new lines, has remained almost stationary since 1950. (See Tables 11 and 12.) In Argentina, textile production in 1958 was 18 per cent less than in 1950; other countries have made only a slight improvement.[6] Apparently, the situation of the textile industry, as well as the very mild growth of the food, drink, and tobacco industries, is linked to bad income distribution, which in turn results from the low productivity of workers in agriculture.

Industry has branched out into new fields: steel, wood pulp, and basic chemicals. This expansion has meant a qualitative and structural change and is bringing about a substantial replacement of imports by supplying intermediate products in wide demand

[6] ECLA, *Economic Bulletin for Latin America*, V, No. 1 (March, 1960), Statistical Supplement, Table 7.

and by initiating the manufacture of machinery and durable consumer goods, which are very important to Latin American industrial development. The emergence of a steel industry, under frequently difficult conditions, has probably been the single event of greatest significance and has made possible a new, mature stage of economic development.

The growth of mining and oil industries has been even more spectacular. Some important characteristics of these activities should be noted. First, mining employs a very small proportion of the population and represents a minimal part of the gross product. Nevertheless, the product per person in mining is extremely high and far superior to that of the rest of industry. Mining is of primary importance as an export activity, and for some countries—Chile, Bolivia, Peru, and Venezuela—it is decisive. But, because it is almost always foreign-owned, it drains off foreign exchange, necessitates special regulations, and gives rise to international disputes. In contrast to Mexico, where mining has stagnated, other countries rich in mineral resources have greatly increased their output since 1950. Production of iron ore has multiplied 5½ times, mainly as a result of expansion in Venezuela, Brazil, and Peru (see Table 13); copper has risen by 39 per cent, thanks to increased output in Peru and Chile; zinc has gone up 34 per cent, primarily in Peru and Argentina; and Mexico leads in production of a new mineral, sulphur. Lead, tin, silver, and gold have made less progress or declined; Peru, however, has increased production of the last three.

Venezuela's dominance of Latin America's petroleum industry is well known. Its 80 per cent share accounts for the 81 per cent increment in total production from 1950 to 1959. (See Table 13.) Mexico ranks second, but its output was less than 10 per cent of Venezuela's during the same period, and it expanded production by only 35 per cent, almost all of which was intended for its domestic market.

Most of the increase in Latin American mining and petroleum production, taken as a unit, can be attributed to Brazil, Peru, and Venezuela. Venezuela alone represents almost 60 per cent of the total, Mexico and Chile each 12 per cent.

From the foregoing, it is clear that the economic growth of Latin America has been not only slow but unevenly distributed. Industrialization, which is undeniably important, has been concentrated in five or six of the most populous countries and has not been uniform. The countries that have experienced considerable industrial expansion have not been able to develop their agriculture at the same rate. In general, agriculture has not been sufficiently stimulated and has been only partially modernized. Mining and petroleum activities have been limited to a few countries, and their growth has had little effect on Latin America's over-all situation. Moreover, like some agricultural products, they have been highly dependent on the fluctuations of the international market.

Nevertheless, there is no reason for pessimism, because the structural change to industrialization is irreversible and leads increasingly to expansions into new industries that directly or indirectly create a demand for primary products. Furthermore, the counterpart of this structural change, greater flexibility in agriculture and livestock raising, can be achieved if consistent policies incorporating well-known technical and social elements are applied to this end.

If economic progress is understood to mean the attainment of greater production with a minimum of resources, then the Latin American experience of the last ten years has provided ample evidence that considerable headway can be made in this direction. It has also demonstrated that growth must be generalized and not restricted to a few sectors. The lag in agriculture and livestock raising can be explained but not justified.

Still, it is not enough to produce without creating the requisite capacity to consume. This is another aspect to consider in judging economic progress. Latin American markets are narrow in not only a physical but a social and economic sense. The already sizable, rapidly growing population does not consume enough to justify new and expanding production because probably more than half, that is about 105 million people, live at a bare subsistence level and cannot yet benefit from modern technical advances. There is almost no country in Latin America that does not have striking inequalities of income, due to the pattern of land distribution, concentration of industry in a few hands, urbanization, inadequate tax policies, and backward social conditions. The great majority of the population receives a small fraction of the income; a select group holds most of the purchasing power. Countries that are exceptions to this unbalanced income distribution are too small to affect the over-all picture. Only today is it beginning to be recognized that uneven income distribution is not just a social problem but also an economic one, because it holds back development.[7] A solution to this problem may be the key to the economic future of Latin America. Its relationship to the lag in agriculture clearly indicates that agriculture must be promoted in most of the countries in order to maintain industrial development. As long as Latin America's economic progress fails to bring substantial income benefits to the farm and industrial workers, who constitute the majority of the population, it is difficult to imagine how growth can be sustained over a long period of time.

Latin America's economy is certainly not autonomous. It always has been and will continue to be linked to the rest of the world, especially to countries that traditionally have imported primary products from Latin America in order to sell it manufactured goods. This situation, which is changing, requires analysis, which will be undertaken in the next chapter.

---

[7] See the author's article, "La distribución de los ingresos y el desarrollo económico," *Política* (Caracas), No. 8, April, 1960.

2. International Trade Trends and Latin America

IT IS POINTLESS simply to go on repeating, as is so common, that Latin America is subject to the fluctuations of international trade; the situation must be analyzed and defined in all its complexities. To state that Latin American economic development has been or is being helped or hampered by the behavior of foreign markets is to say a great deal without really saying anything. It is hardly conceivable that the Latin American economy could have reached its present stage of development without foreign trade. International trade is not an accident but a means by which an economy develops. The degree and scope of its contribution to economic growth and welfare depend on whether buyer or seller is in the stronger position, but as long as there is development, there will be trade.

Development had to begin somewhere in the world, and throughout history its acceleration or deceleration in different countries has brought about changes in the volume and composition of international trade. The less developed countries inevitably tend to link their economies to those of the more advanced countries, which both need their products and are better able to supply their requirements.

Then, is it not more accurate to say that the Latin American economy is subject, not to the fluctuations of international trade, but to the rate and pattern of economic development in the rest of the world, especially in countries with higher per capita income and thus greater demand and purchasing power? If so, attention should be focused on how countries with a high standard of living have evolved and where they are headed. For such an analysis, the traditional "theory of international trade" is hardly useful. It is an analytical method that has prevented consideration of the problem as a whole and as a dynamic process.

Obviously, it is essential to look for the long-term, basic trends. As long as the European economy was predominant and its structure and growth permitted its needs to be met from its own resources, the goods it imported from Latin America created very little real wealth; the precious metals were a means of exchange and an object of greed, but not a raw material for European industry or an article of direct consumption. The industrial revolution, its technical advances, better transportation, and the acceleration of population growth caused shifts in demand and changes in the structure of supply that compelled Europe to import food and raw materials. In responding to Europe's new demands, Latin America entered a new stage of development, which owed much of its momentum to the introduction of modern means of transportation. Next came the impact of the raw-material requirements of United States industrialization. Meanwhile, Latin America benefited from improved techniques —for instance, in the treatment of industrial ores—and changing food habits, especially the growing taste for coffee.

Clearly, industrial countries could not buy from Latin America what it did not produce—manufactured goods—but only the food and raw materials for which it had ample resources and the possibility of establishing adequate means of production. Thus, development in Latin America was a response to that of the more advanced countries—directly, in foreign investment in the production of primary products and exportable foods, and indirectly and less apparently, in the use made of increased domestic income. This process, in no way related to the theory of comparative costs, can be analyzed only in terms of development trends.

Unfortunately, there does not exist, at least to my knowledge, a general study of Latin America's economic evolution since the nineteenth century correlating the growth of exports with the expansion of different branches of industry in Europe and the United States, or with particular shifts in consumer demand. Such a study not only would be interesting in itself, but would give substance to the often repeated thesis of Latin American dependence. Once these relationships, and their cyclical behavior, have been documented, it will be much easier to understand how Latin America's exports are tied to the world economy. Students concerned with the external factors in Latin America's economic growth should worry less about excessive dependence on other countries—these bonds will always exist—and more about the danger that countries of higher productivity and income might become self-sufficient and either halt or reduce their purchases of Latin American products. When more advanced nations no longer need food and raw materials from Latin America, the latter's "dependence" will cease, but so will the drive behind its development.

The foregoing does not condemn Latin America to an endless future of simply trading primary products for manufactured goods. Its own structure of output is changing and will continue to do so, just as the structure of demand in the more advanced countries is being transformed. But it will be many years before an appreciable reduction can be made in the gap between the average level of Latin American productivity and that of Western Europe, the United States, and Canada. Granted, world development should be directed toward narrowing this gap, but as long as it exists, its influence on the nature of international trade must be recognized.

None of the above implies that errors and injustices have never existed or do not exist today in the industrialized nations' trade policy toward the less-developed countries, or that conspiracies, unfair competition, damaging actions by international monopolies, control of transportation media, and the like are unheard of. But in the background, there has always been the reality of an economic evolution that induces uneven development. In addition, anxiety about the international political situation has prompted many countries to create their own source of supply rather than depend on distant producers. Also, important technological changes have affected the relative use and value of different products. Obviously, protectionism is not the result of purely economic causes.

It is interesting to analyze how all these elements have been reflected in the trends and structure of world trade.[1] Until the beginning of this century, the United Kingdom accounted for more than one-fifth of all world imports and, with the rest of Western Europe, absorbed about 60 per cent of the total. Meanwhile, the United States and Canada together received less than 10 per cent. After World War I, the United States and Canada increased their share, which reached 14 per cent in 1937, while the United Kingdom and the rest of Western Europe reduced theirs. (See Table 14.) By 1953, the North American share in imports had grown still larger and that of Western Europe, especially the United Kingdom, still smaller. Thus, during the almost 80 years from 1876 to 1953, the center of gravity of world import demand shifted from Western Europe to the United States —from countries with few natural resources, such as Great Britain, to those with almost limitless potential resources and therefore less need of imports. Nor did the emergence of other industrial powers counteract this phenomenon. The Soviet Union can draw on its own many resources for its industrial development; furthermore, it has never unleashed its latent consumer demand for such articles as coffee and tropical fruit. Japan, like the United Kingdom an importer of food and raw materials, has never had the latter's purchasing power.

Despite these changes in the structure of world trade, Latin America's share of exports rose only slightly over the years. The

---

[1] The analysis that follows and the tables cited therein are based on the valuable work of P. Lamartine Yates, *Forty Years of Foreign Trade* (London, George Allen and Unwin, 1959), Chaps. II and III.

exports of Western Europe, including the United Kingdom, steadily declined, from almost one-half of the total at the beginning of the century to little more than one-third in 1953. The change in the origin of world exports, particularly the relative drop in European exports, makes it surprising that Latin America's share did not increase faster. Between the start of World War I and 1937, it went up from 8 to 10 per cent of the total; by 1953, it had expanded very little more. (See Table 14.) The shares of Africa and Oceania grew faster, and Asia, despite the setback in Japanese trade, also gained ground. Thus, Latin America benefited less from the transfer of the center of gravity to the great United States purchasing area.

The analysis may be carried further by separating trade in primary products from trade in manufactures. In 1913, Latin America supplied nearly 13 per cent of world exports of primary products, and in 1937, this proportion was 16 per cent. In 1953, the ascent was continuing. (See Table 15.) But during the same forty-year span, the combined share of Africa and Oceania almost doubled. In terms of quantum, the growth of Latin American exports lagged considerably behind those of other underdeveloped areas. World trade tripled in volume from 1876 to 1913, but increased by only 50 per cent between 1913 and 1953. Thus, the evolution of the world economy in the latter period was less favorable to exporters of primary products than in the first forty years.

This over-all picture makes it apparent that the United States and Canada, with almost one-fifth of the aggregate, have supplanted the United Kingdom as the principal importer of primary products. Again the question arises: Why has Latin American export trade lagged behind that of other less-developed regions? This is part of the problem, posed earlier, of how the Latin American economy is specifically linked to the economies of industrial countries, a problem that obviously should be studied product by product.

A few hints can be gathered from information already at hand.[2] In 1913, Latin America carried on 21 per cent of the world trade in food, and by 1953, this proportion had grown to 25 per cent. (See Table 16.) But because the income-elasticity of the demand for food is low, the slow rise in European income necessarily had a less favorable effect on Latin America. Practically the only foods imported by the United States were coffee, bananas, and sugar. Latin America advanced only in beverages (that is, coffee) and sugar, and by 1953, it led the world in exports of these, with 64 and 51 per cent, respectively, of the total exports. There is a serious surplus of both these commodities on the market today.

Latin America slid downward mainly in its share of world exports of cereals, livestock products, oilseeds and fats, and fruits and vegetables—precisely the items in which the United States and Canada increased their share of imports between 1913 and 1953. (See Table 16.) This means that Latin America was not supplying either North America's growing needs or Europe's relatively low demand. It may be noted that in 1953–54, the volume of Argentina's wheat exports was only 8 per cent higher than its 1909–13 average forty years earlier, and that it exported 44 per cent less corn and 30 per cent less meat than before World War I. (See Table 17.) Meanwhile, the United States multiplied its meat imports almost by nine, and Italy, Belgium, Holland, the Soviet Union, Sweden, Germany, and other countries became meat importers.[3]

The volume of Latin America's exports of oilseeds and vegetable oils also shrank during these forty years, in both absolute and relative terms (again the case of Argentina), while world imports doubled.[4]

In a discussion of agricultural raw materials—which have become less important in world trade—it is well to remember that the products that have made the most progress in world exports

[2] Yates, *op. cit.*, Chaps. IV and VI.
[3] *Ibid.*, Table 43.
[4] *Ibid.*, Table 52.

since 1913 are rubber, wood pulp, lumber, and tobacco. Latin America has traded very little in rubber and wood pulp. World interchange in textile fibers, which account for nearly half the total of agricultural raw materials, has declined in absolute terms. Nonetheless, Latin America considerably increased its share of total fiber exports, up to nearly 18 per cent in 1953, as against only 6 per cent in 1913. (See Table 16.) Wool exports, which continue to be more important than cotton, remained stationary in Argentina and Uruguay; these two countries, handicapped by hoof-and-mouth disease and Australian competition, actually exported less wool in 1953 than in 1913. (See Table 17.) Significantly, world imports of wool did not rise during those forty years.[5] The plight of cotton has been equally bad or worse. World imports of cotton in 1953 were 13 per cent less than in 1913, owing to reduced purchases by England, Germany, and other countries. But of this declining market,[6] Latin America substantially augmented its share, with exports from Mexico and Brazil displacing those from the United States, Egypt, and India.

The output of minerals and fuels, which play a major role in Latin American exports, has expanded dramatically until recently. Trade in these products in 1953, showed a tremendous increase over the 1913 level, especially in petroleum, tin, zinc, lead, copper, and iron. (See Tables 18, 19, 20, and 21.) Iron was supplied primarily by Sweden, followed by France and North Africa, but Venezuela by 1953 already had reached fourth place and today is probably second. Thus, Venezuela, together with Brazil, has captured for Latin America a sizable share of the growing world demand for a product that is beginning to be in short supply in many industrial countries. Copper is an import necessity for both the United States and Europe. Chile, the world's second-largest exporter of copper after central Africa, continues to expand its output and is the mainstay behind Latin America's present production of one-third of the world total.

[5] *Ibid.*, Table 62.
[6] *Ibid.*, Table 61.

The increase in Chilean exports has scored a substantial gain for Latin America. Similar advances have been made in lead; over the forty-year period, exports have been shifting from Spain to Mexico and lately Peru.

Latin America produces 25 per cent of the world's zinc, which is chiefly imported by Europe and the United States in the form of zinc concentrates. From 1913 to 1953, Mexico and Peru increased their exports of zinc concentrates at the expense of Australia.[7] The swiftly rising demand for zinc is expected to continue for some time to come. On the other hand, the weak trend in tin has had an adverse effect on the export trade of Latin America and its leading tin producer, Bolivia.

The spectacular expansion of petroleum—1955 world imports of crude oil were six times the 1929 level and those of refined oil were three times that level—has caused an extraordinary change in Latin America's trade structure. In 1955, Latin America, mainly Venezuela, accounted for 44 per cent of all refined-oil exports and 40 per cent of all crude-oil exports. However, in the last fifteen to twenty years, Europe, which has always been the principal customer for both crude and refined oil, has turned to the Middle East for its supply.

The foregoing data are important not only as historical background but as a basis for appraising the future. Of the total value of Latin America's exports, more than 25 per cent is represented by petroleum and derivatives; 18 to 22 per cent by coffee; 9 per cent by sugar; 4 per cent by cotton; 2.5 per cent by copper; and 2.4 per cent by iron ore. (See Tables 25, 26, and 28.) These six products make up almost two-thirds of the value of all exports. Add twelve more products—meat, hides and skins, cacao, wheat, corn (maize), tobacco, wool, quebracho, lead, tin, zinc, and nitrates—and almost three-quarters of the total value is accounted for. Every product on this list, with the possible exception of iron ore, faces grave market difficulties arising from serious malad-

[7] The principal exporters of zinc metal are Belgium and Canada.

justments between world demand and potential world exports. Naturally, prices have reflected this situation. It is estimated that the export prices of 17 commodities, roughly those listed above, have declined an average of 9 per cent from their 1950 level and 16 per cent from their 1955 level. (See Table 23.) The prices of tropical products, particularly coffee and cotton, and nonferrous metals, chiefly lead and zinc, have fallen more than 25 per cent, many of them below their 1948 level. These immediate factors of actual and potential instability must be considered along with the long-term growth rates and protectionist policies of the various industrial countries. At present, Latin America's economic prospects are threatened by a decline in price or by over-supply of most of its export products.

Nevertheless, the more distant future may be brighter, at least for some products. A primary factor in this is the outlook for the world economy and the repercussions it is likely to have on Latin America's trade, or more specifically, its leading products.

The United States spends about $4 billion a year to purchase almost one-half of Latin America's exports—chiefly petroleum and coffee, followed by copper, iron ore, lead, and cacao. (See Table 24.) From 1946–48 to 1955–57, the United States economy expanded an average of 3.8 per cent per annum. Some projections assume a growth rate of 4.3 to 4.5 per cent until 1970.[8] This implies that the United States will increase sizably its imports of certain Latin American products, especially minerals, such as iron ore and copper, in which its resources are approaching depletion, and petroleum, for which its demand will probably continue buoyant. (See Table 27.) The prices of these commodities are expected to remain steady. On the other hand, United States purchases of coffee in the next decade are not expected to exceed previous levels. Its low rate of population growth makes it impossible for the United States to absorb any appreciable part of

[8] Projections of the National Planning Association, quoted by Louis O. Delwart, *The Future of Latin American Exports to the United States: 1965 and 1970* (Washington, D.C., 1960), p. 14.

the coffee surpluses in the next few years. The United States demand for other products may increase, but these do not play so important a role. Although they may be crucial to certain countries, they do not count for much in the aggregate. At best, United States growth, which may not be so rapid as some projections indicate, will benefit Latin America only in its rising demand for minerals (see Table 27); U.S. imports of coffee and a number of foodstuffs will expand slowly and with fluctuating prices.

An unfavorable trend for exporters of primary products is the declining ratio of consumption of raw materials to gross product experienced in industrial countries. In Canada and the United States,[9] these ratios are estimated to have dropped from 8.19 and 6.07 per cent, respectively, in 1926–28 to 7.13 and 5.10 per cent in 1955–57, and they are expected to shrink to 6.30 and 4.71 per cent by 1980. (See Table 31.) In the United States, this decline has been more marked in fuels, and in Canada, in lumber and pulp.

Western Europe, which takes 30 per cent of Latin America's exports, generally has shown a higher rate of economic growth than the United States. Its future impact on Latin America may be important in several products, including petroleum, iron ore, copper, zinc, sulphur, coffee, cacao, and wool. Again, prospects are better for minerals and petroleum than for other products. (See Tables 29 and 30.) But, despite their brisk over-all growth, European countries do not expand proportionately their purchases of agricultural primary products. Food has a low income-elasticity, agriculture is highly protected, and substitutes have been developed for many raw materials.[10] In Europe, the outlook is not very promising for Latin American cotton, meat, cereals, oilseeds and fats, sugar, and fruits. In many instances, it will be difficult to overcome the preference given to African and Asian

[9] Wilbert G. Fritz, *The Future of Industrial Raw Materials in North America* (National Planning Association, Canadian-American Committee [Washington, D.C., 1960]), pp. 17–18.

[10] Economic Commission for Europe, *Economic Survey of Europe in 1957*, Chap. V.

suppliers. Furthermore, Western Europe's population is expected to increase only 0.6 per cent per annum.

The 20 per cent of Latin American exports not sold to the United States or Western Europe is evenly divided between Latin America itself, on the one hand, and Japan and Eastern Europe, on the other. In the last few years, trade with Japan has expanded considerably, especially in cotton, sugar, and wool.[11] But despite the very rapid growth forecast for the Japanese economy, the sum total of these figures does not alter the general outlook.

Although Latin America's exports to the Soviet Union and other countries of Eastern Europe have recently increased, their volume, at least until 1959, has not been significant.[12] There is no basis on which to calculate their future growth. The Canadian market is also of little consequence.

Taking into account the various studies on the subject, the expansion of Latin American trade, as linked to the growth of other parts of the world—principally the United States and Europe, where it now sends nearly 80 per cent of its exports—can be anticipated as follows: a substantial increase in exports of minerals, metals, and petroleum; a slight expansion in food exports (in the long run, this will depend primarily on what happens to coffee); and a somewhat higher increment in exports of agricultural raw materials, which in any case represent only a small proportion of the total. (See the ECLA projections cited in Table 28.)

These estimates usually omit the possible effect of tourism

[11] "Recent Developments and Prospects in Trade Between Latin America and Japan," *Economic Bulletin for Latin America,* II, No. 1 (February, 1957).

[12] ECLA, "Preliminary Notes on Latin American Trade with the Countries with Centrally Planned Economies," *Economic Survey of Latin America 1957,* Annex to Chap. III. See also *Soviet Bloc Latin American Activities and Their Implications for United States Foreign Policy,* a Study prepared at the request of the Subcommittee on Foreign Relations, United States Senate, by the Corporation for Economic and Industrial Research (February 8, 1960). Reprinted in *United States–Latin America Relations, Compilation of Studies* (U.S. Senate, 86th Congress, 2d Session, Doc. No. 125. [Washington, D.C., Government Printing Office, August 31, 1960]).

on Latin America's future foreign-exchange earnings. At present, tourism yields a net balance of nearly $550 million, which is not large in relation to total export trade, but considered as an individual earner, is in fourth place after petroleum, coffee, and sugar. Most of this income goes to Mexico (along its borders) and a lesser amount goes to Haiti, Panama, and Uruguay. (See Table 32.) Argentina, Brazil, and Venezuela have negative travel balances. Tourism, at least in Mexico, is expanding faster than any export product, and in ten years will probably be a major element in the general picture of Latin America's external demand. It will be determined primarily by the rate and level of disposable income in the United States, although in time it should benefit significantly from tourism of other countries.

Latin America's dependence, through trade and tourism, on the economic development of other countries will continue indefinitely. It would be to Latin America's advantage to diversify both export products and markets and to send abroad products with a higher degree of processing, but these would not essentially alter the problem. For Latin America to increase sales to countries that have not been important customers, these countries must grow more rapidly and want Latin American products. This is even true of Latin America itself, as a market. Herein lies the value of the present free-trade zone and the future Latin American common market.[13]

Dependence involves other problems: on the one hand, price fluctuations; on the other, foreign investments and credits. Price fluctuations are particularly serious because they discourage the investments necessary to augment exports, they frequently have very unfavorable repercussions on other aspects of the domestic economy, as well as on financial conditions, and they bring about production cycles that intensify the imbalance of supply and demand. It is evident that anything that can be done to avoid or moderate fluctuations will in the long run benefit Latin

[13] See Chap. 10.

America. The practice of calculating what Latin America "loses" every time prices fall does not seem to be a very useful analytical method, since what is "no longer earned" is not always "lost"; an economic analysis would also have to estimate the effect that continued high prices would have had on the volume of output and exports. A sharp rise in export prices can be as harmful as a decline, because it may lead to inflationary disturbances and create incentives for production on a scale that is subsequently not justified. But it cannot be denied that the Latin American economy would be strengthened if prices were less erratic and if suitable international agreements were adopted to this end.[14]

Another problem presented by Latin America's economic dependence concerns the terms of trade, i.e., the ratio of average prices of exports to those of imports. It is not exclusively a problem of underdeveloped countries. Great Britain is very sensitive to the terms of trade, as is natural for a country whose imports not only are essential to the functioning and growth of its economy, but also constitute a significant cost factor. Many objections of a statistical nature have been raised over the measuring of the terms of trade, chiefly on the grounds that changes in the composition of exports and imports influence indices and that the quality of products varies with the passage of time. But there is no question that over the last eighty years, export prices of primary products in general have dropped in relation to those of manufactured goods. Between 1876–80 and 1896–1900—that is, in about the final quarter-century—the prices of primary products declined by 26 per cent, and by 1913 they had not returned to their original level. In the same period, prices of manufactures fell by only 7 per cent, and by 1913 they had recovered to a level slightly higher than the original. (See Table 22.) In the forty years from 1913 to 1953, average prices of exports of primary products went up 136 per cent, but those of manufactures rose 175 per cent. Thus, for about eighty years the terms of trade

[14] See Chap. 5.

have been moving against primary products, and in the last forty years alone they have worsened by 16 per cent. Latin America, of course, has been adversely affected by this trend; from 1953 to 1959, it suffered an additional drop of 21 per cent because of a slump in average export prices and an upswing in import prices. (See Table 23.)

This problem has been widely discussed in recent years. In the United Nations, hundreds of man-hours and stacks of paper have been devoted to the question of whether there should not be more "just" or "equitable" terms of trade. Obviously, this kind of discussion leads to no solution and only turns the problem into a political issue. The problem of fluctuating export prices in world markets is more susceptible to treatment. But the terms of trade, which derive from the very structure of the world economy —the development rates of different regions and their relative levels of industrialization and technical progress—cannot be remedied by price regulation. Once again it is apparent that a country is at a disadvantage because it is insufficiently developed and not because it has to trade with the rest of the world.

Transportation is considered to be another factor in the dependence of the Latin American economy, because of the control exercised by the countries supplying most of the shipping and the protection accorded their fleets. There is no doubt that Latin American countries could economize on foreign exchange by employing their own merchant marines more extensively. Dependence could be reduced in this way. However—and this is not always recognized—the individual exporter does not necessarily save money by shipping under his national flag. In any case, he must pay freight charges that are usually fixed by international agreement. This is a subject that merits further study.

Finally, the Latin American economies are dependent on those of the rest of the world because they need to import equipment, machinery, raw materials, some consumer goods, and even basic foodstuffs. In this case, the relationship is of a different nature, because for Latin America the question is not whether industrial countries are interested in selling it equipment or machinery; in fact, the latter's elasticity of supply seems to present no difficulties. The problem for Latin America is that it must acquire foreign exchange, by exports or loans, to pay for its imports. If the amount is insufficient, economic development can be held back. Hence the basic importance of the roles played by all aspects of Latin América's foreign trade and by foreign financing in this region's future economic development.

3. Monetary and Financial Imbroglios[1]

IT IS CURIOUS that other underdeveloped regions of the world have not undergone and do not today experience the kind of financial and monetary difficulties that seem to be typical of economic development in Latin America. Countries such as the Philippines and Indonesia cannot really be said to have relative monetary stability, but they both suffered directly from World War II and one of them is still not properly organized as a fully independent country. Pakistan and India, for example, have financial problems. Exchange restrictions have been imposed in Egypt. But nowhere outside Latin America have there been the long periods of financial confusion that have recently afflicted Brazil, Chile, Bolivia, Argentina, Paraguay, and Uruguay. What is there about Latin America that predisposes it to inflation and financial difficulties?

Undoubtedly, a partial explanation can be found in history: the political instability of the nineteenth century, which has still not disappeared, and the nature of the institutions inherited from independence, which are not all conducive to good financial order. It may be assumed that in its "zeal to develop," Latin America has undertaken more than has been justified by its financial resources and savings. But Canada has always been just as intent on expansion; yet its development has come about under comparatively stable conditions. Furthermore, in Latin America,

1 "Imbroglio" means confusion, complication; also, a serious misunderstanding; and in a figurative sense, an embarrassing situation. All these meanings are pertinent.

as elsewhere, the lack of domestic savings has been filled by foreign capital and credits. Without going any deeper into the subject, it appears that the financial and monetary instability of nineteenth-century Latin America was due in large part to civil conflicts, frequent wars, the isolation of large areas, and periodical crises in exports of primary products. The special factor operating in Latin America and not in other underdeveloped regions is probably the social structure and other elements that influence the general level of productivity.

Its troubled history left Latin America with a substantial foreign debt, which remained undiminished in spite of the upsurge in mining exports during the late nineteenth and early twentieth centuries, and the boom that followed World War I. Some foreign debts were contracted to finance specific projects, such as railway construction; others were made simply to defray current government expenditures or to pay the cost of wars. Many of the debts were for amounts much greater than the sums actually received. When payments were suspended, so much interest-due accumulated that the total debt became unredeemable, because of the frequent breakdown in the debtor's ability to pay. In the 1920's, credits were granted rather liberally to Latin America at the same time that efforts were being made to build up a system of modern banking around a conventional central bank. These monetary reforms and the financial improvements they connoted were part of the final, inglorious stage of the international gold standard. The great world economic crisis that began in 1929 exploded all that had been attempted or remained of monetary orthodoxy. From that moment, it was a currency free-for-all, in which no country came out ahead.

It is well known that the depression of 1929–33 had a drastic effect on the volume of world trade in primary products, as well as on prices. It had, however, an even stronger impact on trade in manufactures.[2] And this decline, linked to reduced industrial

[2] As had also occurred during the depression of 1890–93. See Yates, *op. cit.*, pp. 39–45.

production, spreading unemployment, and lowered incomes, meant that the principal industrial countries would take many years to recover economically. In 1940, at the outset of World War II, almost no industrial country had completely emerged from the doldrums of the thirties. In 1938, the volume of world exports of manufactures was still 19 per cent below that of 1929 and, in fact, barely equal to the 1913 level. On the other hand, the 1938 quantum of exports of primary products was only 6 per cent lower than in 1929, and was 24 per cent higher than in 1913.[3]

During the depression, exports of primary products fluctuated less in volume than did manufactures, but varied more in price. This is why countries exporting raw materials and foods earned less foreign exchange. Actually, these countries suffered considerably from the crisis of the thirties because, in addition to the above factors, their domestic situations were heavily dependent on their foreign trade. Their balance of payments deficits had deflationary repercussions and the gloomy international outlook discouraged domestic investment. Any governmental attempts to maintain aggregate demand by increasing public expenditure gave rise to budget imbalances, which were met by issuing new currency, and aggravated the balance of payments disequilibria by stimulating imports. The delay in the recovery of the industrial countries, together with the efforts of the underdeveloped countries to protect their foreign exchange earnings by expanding the volume of their exports, prolonged the period of weakened prices for primary products. Moreover, in certain products, such as coffee, tin, rubber, copper, and nitrate, the gap between supply and demand dated from an earlier period and was simply widened by the depression. Under such conditions, it is not surprising that underdeveloped countries found it difficult to preserve their external monetary stability. No short-term credit

---

[3] Even in 1948, the *quantum* of world exports of manufactures was only 19 per cent above the 1913 level, and that of primary products was just 12 per cent higher than before the war. *Ibid.*, taken from Tables 11 and 12.

was available, nor were there any appreciable inflows of long-term investment or credit with which to pay for part of the imports. These problems induced many countries to adopt rather unorthodox methods to finance industrialization and increase public expenditures in basic development projects.

World War II was for most underdeveloped countries, and especially for Latin America, a two-edged sword. Exports of primary products expanded in volume and improved in price. But this mounting demand, which under any other circumstances would have benefited Latin America, could not be met without a rise in prices at home, because there was obviously a restricted supply of machinery and intermediate products. Consequently, the pendulum swung to the other extreme, and external monetary stability was achieved at the cost of severe internal inflation. The postwar period brought new readjustments, because the declining world demand for primary products coincided with the growing needs of underdeveloped countries for machinery and other manufactures, which had gone up in price. Again, conditions were unfavorable to economic development with monetary stability, and they were only partially eased by capital inflow and foreign loans. Since then, prices of primary products have remained weak, intensifying Latin America's monetary and financial difficulties. Moreover, a greater export volume of primary products no longer serves to offset low prices—in the case of such commodities as wheat and meat, because it has not occurred; and in the case of coffee, lead, and petroleum, because it would bring down prices still further. From 1938 to 1956, the world export volume of manufactures went up by 131 per cent, while that of primary products rose by only 48 per cent.[4] This disparity can be attributed largely to the postwar recovery of Europe, the pressure there and in other areas of machinery and equipment requirements, and the substitution of domestic for imported primary products.

[4] *Ibid.*, Table 12.

Moreover, economic development itself has tended to be inflationary; that is, it has contributed to a steady rise in the price level. This has been clearly demonstrated in Latin America. Economic development has implied, in the first place, self-examination: the entertainment of doubts that devoting real resources solely to exports would result in a general rise in the employment and income level of the population. In the second place, it has involved long-term investments in sectors like transport, electric power, agriculture, education, and health, which are essential to growth but do not yield immediate results. In the third place, such programs have generally required a higher ratio of investment, or that part of the national product not made available for consumption but allocated to enlarging productive capacity. In the fourth place, it has been necessary to give priority to industrialization as a way to absorb surplus farm population, provide better-paid employment, exploit natural resources in behalf of the nation and promote a broader utilization of them, and reserve often precarious foreign-exchange earnings for purchasing only the most essential imports. Until higher levels of development are reached, domestic investment will need to incorporate a substantial amount of imports of machinery and equipment, intermediate products, and technical services.

In the early stages of this process, incomes are created immediately, but a period of time must elapse before output increases. During this time, the expanded wages and salaries are spent on available goods and services. If domestic production is not yet sufficient to meet demand, part of the income generated will be used to purchase imports, even of essential goods. If imports cannot be increased or if they cost more because of external factors, expenditures tend to raise domestic prices. This is the source of the inflation that is linked to economic development.

Actually, the process is much more complicated. Economic development produces considerable changes in structure and important shifts in occupation. The people entering urban industrial occupations and the farmer benefiting by investment in rural areas, will change the pattern of their demand: they will consume more and better food, and they will spend more money on clothing and other necessities, and even on amusements. Certain types of demand grow more rapidly than others, outstripping production. In particular, food supply usually lags behind demand, largely because increasing it requires changes in the system of land tenure, additional investments, improved farming methods, agricultural extension and market-orientation services, more profitable prices, and social reforms—all of which can only be achieved slowly. A developing country often has to import even basic foods.

As a country proceeds toward industrialization, it needs to be protected by tariffs and exchange and other regulations, owing to its initial lower productivity and to prevent ruinous competition from foreign products. This is another factor that raises prices. Furthermore, industrial progress may be hindered by lack of electric power, fuel, transportation, construction materials, technical services, skilled labor, good administrators or managers, and effective government policies.

If a drop in the prices of its export goods shrinks the foreign-exchange earnings of an industrializing country at the same time that its demand for imports is growing, its balance-of-payments disequilibrium may compel it to take defensive measures to reduce expenditures on all or less essential imports. These measures may include higher tariffs, direct import control by permits, exchange control and varying exchange rates for different import categories, or open or masked devaluation of its currency vis-à-vis the rest of the world. The exchange shortage may be so serious that even imports of equipment and other indispensable products will be subject to control or exchange surcharges. All restricted import articles become more expensive. Thus, the consequences of a lack of foreign-exchange earnings also contribute to the rise in prices that accompanies economic development.

All these factors are today called "structural," that is, they originate in the basic economic structure of a country and of its foreign trade.[5] Development is accompanied by price rises because it brings about different growth rates for different segments of aggregate demand, and the structure of supply (principally, domestic production, but also imports) is not sufficiently flexible to adapt to changes in the structure of demand without incurring dislocations such as shortages, bottlenecks, and specific cases of excess demand, which are in turn transmitted to other points.

The degree of monopoly in industrial and other activities is also important, because it encourages enterprises to maintain high prices and even raise them in the face of particular increases in demand. In most Latin American countries, markets are so limited that quasi-monopolies are easily formed and then strengthened by tariff and exchange protection.

Uneven income distribution is another undesirable factor in the inflationary process, because it channels investments into activities supplying prosperous urban sectors, and away from industries producing general consumer goods, for which the market thus remains limited. Income concentration leads to the importation of luxury articles and other expenditures that make no contribution to development. It implies, moreover, that savings are misused and, of course, badly distributed.

[5] The "structuralist" explanation of inflation is gaining followers, even though antimonetary arguments are sometimes exaggerated. Structuralist ideas are shared by some studies of the ECLA and of a number of individual Latin American economists. See the admirable summary of the controversy between structuralists and monetarists in David Felix's "An Alternative View of the Monetarist-Structuralist Controversy," in *Latin American Issues: Essays and Comments,* ed. Albert O. Hirschman (New York, Twentieth Century Fund, 1961). See also in the same volume, Joseph Grunwald's "The 'Structuralist' School on Price Stability and Development: The Chilean Case." Grunwald's article has a very complete bibliography. Also recommended, although it does not entirely conform to a purely structuralist point of view, is Raúl Prebisch's "Economic Development or Monetary Stability: The False Dilemma," *Economic Bulletin for Latin America* (Santiago de Chile), VI, No. 1 (March, 1961). An excellent theoretical review of the whole question is Dudley Seer's "A Theory of Inflation and Growth in Underdeveloped Economies Based on the Experience of Latin America," *Oxford Economic Papers,* XIV, No. 2 (June, 1962), 173–95.

Finally, the investment program itself may be unbalanced. Concern over basic problems may lead to a disproportionate amount of investment in long-term projects that do not yield results for some time. The planning of certain public or private investment projects may be so poor that long and costly modifications or additions may be necessary before such projects can operate efficiently. And frequently there is too little coordination between the different sectors of the public investment projects, for example, agriculture and transportation, or between public and private investment programs.

In brief, economic development creates structural imbalances that tend to induce somewhat higher prices. A moderate rise in prices would be acceptable to all social sectors if it were accompanied by a faster increase in real income, an appreciable degree of industrialization, a significant improvement in agricultural output, and generally, a broadening of the nation's means of production and a more equitable distribution of its income. But in many of the principal Latin American countries, the rise in prices has not been moderate; on the contrary, there have been several cases of runaway inflation, some others of considerable inflation, and many instances of external monetary disturbances. Moreover, the countries experiencing the severest inflation have not always been those with the highest rate of development.

In just the ten years from 1950 to 1960, the over-all price level in Bolivia went up 91½ times, or at a compound annual rate of 57.3 per cent. (See Tables 33 and 34.)[6] In Chile, it rose 21 times, or by 36.4 per cent a year. Prices in Paraguay increased 16½ times, or 33.3 per cent each year. In Argentina, the price level was multiplied by 11½, for an annual increase of 27.7 per cent. In Brazil, it went up 7 times, or 21.8 per cent per annum. The price level in Uruguay rose more than 4½ times or by 16.7 per cent a year. These are cases of acute inflation.

In Bolivia, Chile, and Paraguay, prices increased more rapidly

[6] In what follows, reference is made to indices of wholesale prices or of the cost of living, whichever is more representative.

between 1950 and 1955 (inflation had begun long before), and in the subsequent five-year period inflation diminished and was almost checked. Argentina, Brazil, Chile, and Uruguay have suffered a recurrence of inflation recently, especially in the last two years. Brazil's prices rose 35 per cent in 1960, and an additional 34 per cent in the first half of 1961.[7] In Argentina, prices rose by 27 per cent in 1960, and by July, 1961, they had increased another 15 per cent. On the other hand, Bolivia's price level went up by only 12 per cent in 1960, and by another 6 per cent through the middle of 1961. In Chile, prices rose by just 6 per cent in 1960, and not at all in 1961. Paraguay seemed to have inflation temporarily under control in 1960, as price climbed by only 11 per cent, but they soared by 27 per cent in the first half of 1961.

There has been far less inflation in the remaining Latin American countries. Peru stands out, with a 1960 price level 2.6 times that of 1950, and an average annual increment of 10.2 per cent. The rate of increase accelerated in the final five years. In 1960, it was 18 per cent, but it leveled off in 1961. Over the ten-year period, domestic prices in Colombia and Mexico went up at an average annual rate of 7 per cent, reaching roughly twice their original level. In Mexico the rate of increment has been slowing down, but in Colombia it has stepped up in the last five years. In 1960, prices in Mexico and Colombia rose by only 5 and 4 per cent respectively, but by July, 1961, Mexico's price level had remained stable, while Colombia's had mounted another 10 per cent. In Nicaragua, prices climbed somewhat less than in Peru, Mexico, and Colombia. Almost no inflation has occurred in Costa Rica, El Salvador, Guatemala, Honduras, Ecuador, the Dominican Republic, and Venezuela, where a yearly price rise of less than 3 per cent is not a problem. In Mexico and Colombia, where inflation has been mild, the rate of economic development has been rather high. In Brazil, where there has been runaway inflation, the economy has also developed rapidly. But

[7] The price rises later got out of hand, stimulated by the political crisis of September, 1961.

in four countries that have suffered acute inflation—Bolivia, Chile, Paraguay, and Argentina—economic growth has been slow. In Venezuela, a country that has had little inflation, development has been spectacular. And in several countries there has been neither inflation nor development.

Clearly, it is not easy to correlate the two variables: price levels and real per capita income. Excessive inflation is certainly undesirable, because it impedes orderly growth. But the case of Brazil, apparently an exception, can be explained in two ways. Brazil is the country that has done the most to promote industrial development, and it has never made its domestic growth subject to its balance-of-payments equilibrium. When it has lacked foreign exchange, it has simply imported on credit, and used subsequent loans to refinance its outstanding debts. The case of Venezuela, a country that has had rapid economic growth and mild inflation, must be qualified. Its expansion has been concentrated almost exclusively in its petroleum industry; moreover, foreign exchange earnings from the latter have enabled it to solve supply rigidities by importing whatever has been necessary, including all kinds of consumer goods. But Venezuela has neglected the agricultural and industrial sectors of its economy. Mexico offers the case of a country that has developed considerably, although to a lesser degree in agriculture, and that over the years has managed to prevent its price level from rising unduly in the face of changes in its structure. It has been aided by substantial foreign exchange earnings from tourism and a fairly large net income of long-term capital from abroad. The mildness of Mexico's inflation can be explained not only by the relative flexibility of its economy, but by the fact that its comparatively conservative monetary and wage policies have not tended to spread price rises.

In conjunction with changes in structure, the nature of monetary and wage policies has aggravated inflation in several South American countries. Indisputably, the absence of a true central bank in Brazil, the ineffectiveness of the central banks in Chile and Uruguay, and unrestrained budget deficits in all three

countries—just as in Argentina, Paraguay, and Bolivia—have
meant that insufficient amounts of savings have been directed
toward financing important sectors of demand that have expanded
steadily. Lack of an adequate tax system has undoubtedly intensified inflationary trends (this statement also applies to Mexico).
In addition to the foregoing institutional deficiencies, the countries most severely afflicted with inflation have had to cope with
different groups fighting to recover as quickly as possible their
respective losses in purchasing power or their shares of available goods and services. Finally, at various times, psychological
and speculative factors have induced inflation. The case of Bolivia
involves other and still more difficult circumstances that cannot
be gone into here.

Given the complexity of inflation in Latin America, there can
be no simple solutions like those so often proposed by persons
who have never bothered to study the facts. Certainly, any good
technical solution would have to take into account the many
noneconomic factors. But even on technical grounds, it is evident
that a stabilization policy that does not attack all aspects of inflation cannot succeed. There is the example of Chile, where a
crude, inadequate attempt at stabilization led to economic stagnation—the equivalent of drowning a baby to stop its crying.
As Chile's leading economists had foreseen, the country achieved
"neither stability nor development."[8] If the decisive factors in a
situation are internal, then the points of rigidity in production—
especially food, energy, fuel, and transport—should be relieved
by a well-thought-out and properly financed investment policy.
If a balance-of-payments squeeze is a principal cause of structural
difficulties, then, before taking any other measures, it is essential

---

[8] Title of a book by Aníbal Pinto (Santiago, 1960). See Grunwald, *op. cit.*
A penetrating analysis of the Chilean situation will be found in Osvaldo
Sunkel's article "Inflation in Chile: An Unorthodox Approach," *International Economic Papers* (London, Macmillan, 1960), No. 10, pp. 107–31. A recent account by Albert O. Hirschman in *Journeys Towards Progress* (New
York, Twentieth Century Fund, 1963), Chap. III, provides unusual insight
into the manifold political, social, and economic influences at work in Chile.

to secure the requisite long-, medium-, or short-term foreign credit; again, it may be advisable or even preferable to shore up export prices through an international agreement or other means. If an important role is played by the mechanisms that spead price rises, the other measures adopted cannot yield the desired results until instruments of monetary and fiscal control are modified and money and wage policies are improved. In any case, development programs need to be supplemented by constant improvements in the tools of monetary control, the tax and exchange systems, and the methods used to enlarge capital markets and channel savings toward the priority types of investment. In turn, development programs need to be drawn up with more foresight and carried out with more care. Once again, it is evident that problems in development are not isolated but part of an indivisible whole.

In many Latin American countries, the actual financial situation of the government is hard to appraise, because of the existence of a considerable parastatal sector that, although partially self-financed, receives funds from the government and issues securities on the capital market or obtains financing from banks or from abroad. Frequently it is stated that the government's budget is met by its tax revenue, with no explanation of the degree to which the parastatal sector has obtained financing from resources that in origin and impact amount to a budget deficit. In countries like Argentina, the losses suffered by government enterprises have a very adverse effect on the financial situation; the latter cannot be remedied by simply trying to offset such losses out of tax revenues, but only by reducing them. Furthermore, these losses often derive from the excessively low rates authorized for public utilities during inflationary periods, a mistaken policy that contributes to the inflationary spiral. In several other countries, the social security systems receive sums, similar to taxes, in excess of their current expenditures or possibilities of investment, and they make these surpluses available to other elements of the public sector in the form of loans. On the whole, most countries, especially those suffering from hyperinflation, probably have had aggregate deficits comprising both governmental and parastatal entities. In quite a few countries, military and other nonproductive expenditures constitute a high proportion—from 20 to 30 per cent—of the government's total budget. A reduction in these would free funds for investment in productive activities and also would ease the balance-of-payments situation. There is no doubt that savings could be effected in different branches of the public administration of many Latin American countries. But at the core of the problem lies the tax system, which in most countries is insufficient, inadequate, and based on outdated theories.

According to a comparative study made in 1955—apparently, there is none more recent—the tax burden in Latin America, except for Venezuela and Argentina, was less than 15 per cent of the gross national product during the 1950–54 period; in several countries, including Honduras, Brazil, and Mexico, it was no more than 10 per cent.[9] By contrast, the tax burden in the United States is about 20 per cent of the gross product, and in several European countries it is nearly 30 per cent. If the rest of the public sector is taken into account in Latin America, the percentages are increased, but in no case are they large. Tax systems have probably become less effective with inflation, especially when they have depended on tax receipts that do not increase proportionately with the rise in prices. Inefficient tax systems have accentuated the inflationary process and helped perpetuate forms of consumption that unfavorably affect the balance of payments, or do not contribute to economic development; moreover, because they are regressive, they generate further price rises.

During the Punta del Este Conference, discussions of the problems of economic development in Latin America stressed the

[9] See ECLA, *Economic Survey of Latin America, 1955,* Part II, Government income and expenditures, 1947–54.

urgency of tax reform.[10] It must be understood that, apart from its effect on the financial situation of Latin American governments, tax reform would have economic consequences encouraging to development (provided, of course, that development programs constantly improve). An expanding economy can tolerate a heavier tax burden, particularly one aimed at business profits and personal income. It is obvious that an economy progresses because of the volume and quality of its public and private investments, and not because of its low taxes. If too little is collected in taxes, investment and public expenditures may be insufficient to promote development, or it may become necessary to resort to deficit financing, which would reinforce the inflationary bias of a program of economic development and encourage the kind of open inflation that still prevails in several Latin American countries.

In conclusion, this is an attempt not to justify inflation in Latin America but to explain it and make clear that it is not simply the result of bad government, as is often surmised. Inflation arises partly from Latin America's foreign trade difficulties, which are linked to changes in the world economy; partly from structural changes caused by economic development itself; and partly from mistaken or inadequate monetary and financial policies, or the lack of a well-defined policy, or even an ineffective tax policy. Economic development with stability cannot be achieved by depending exclusively on internal measures designed to curb aggregate demand or sectional demand, or to make domestic output more flexible; neither can it be achieved on the basis of foreign loans alone. Today, it appears that the solution must be a manifold and, above all, forceful one.

---

[10] Two subsequent meetings of experts under OAS and ECLA auspices, one on tax administration and the other on tax policy, made specific recommendations.

4. The Participation of Foreign Capital

BROADLY SPEAKING, "foreign capital" means any transfer of funds from one country to another that does not involve current movements of goods or services. This definition includes as foreign capital any exchange that enters a country without a specific purpose, for example, simply to be deposited in a bank. In general, it is assumed that foreign capital entering a country to participate in economic development, that is, in productive activities, is a long-term transfer for the purpose of acquiring or creating a physical asset. With foreign capital added to domestic savings, a country can increase its output beyond that permitted by its own resources, even though in the process it goes into debt to the rest of the world.

It is well known that foreign-capital transfers enable the borrowing country to import more than it exports to the extent of the amount of exchange it receives. From the standpoint of national expenditure, the use of foreign capital makes it possible to offer the community more goods and services than can be obtained from domestic output. Therefore, if a country has decided to allocate a higher percentage of its available resources to expanding its output and speeding up its economic development, the additional real resources represented by foreign capital can play an important role in accelerating growth. But unless a country is determined to devote more of its efforts to capital formation, funds from abroad will only lead to increased consumption.

The foregoing makes clear that development is helped not by

the volume of foreign capital, but by the uses assigned to the sum total of all available national and imported resources. If at the same time that foreign capital is invested in a specific industry or some other productive activity, domestic resources are wasted in nonproductive activities or spent on consumption or sent abroad, the former will have contributed little or nothing, even though factories and mines may be the visible result of its investment. Paradoxically, foreign capital employed in the purchase of foodstuffs, which are a prime example of consumer goods, can make a valuable contribution to economic development by enabling a country to divert a substantial percentage of its real resources to productive investment.

In this context, it does not matter whether a country receives foreign capital as money or as goods, or goods as machinery or as food, provided it can take the measures necessary to raise its investment ratio. In actual practice, capital transfers from a highly developed to an underdeveloped country, directly or through an international financial agency, are mainly in the form of technical services and capital goods, such as machinery and equipment, rather than consumer goods, as a safeguard against wasteful expenditures. Unless the underdeveloped country makes wise use of all resources, both internal and external, at its disposal, capital transfers in the form of machinery do not guarantee the desired result.

Another point to remember is that the country receiving foreign capital incurs a debt that must be paid back with interest or dividends; therefore, it should accept such resources from abroad only if it can utilize them to advance its development and improve its future balance of payments. Foreign capital ought to make a positive contribution to the country's growth and create the means, through increased exports or reduced imports, with which to amortize it and pay the interest on past borrowing. Because it is impossible to predict how long this process will take —perhaps a very long time—it may be assumed that there will also be a long period of net movement or flow of capital from the more developed to the less developed countries.

This chapter so far has undertaken to give only an economic explanation of the role foreign capital has played and may be expected to play in Latin America's economic development. Capital movements actually present many other aspects, both social and political, depending on whether they take the form of private capital, unrestricted loans, private, official foreign or international credits, or subsidies or grants; whether they originate in North America, Europe, or the Soviet Union; whether they are used for investment in mining, petroleum, agriculture, manufacturing, or distribution; whether the borrowers or debtors are governments, public utilities, state corporations, or private enterprises; whether or not they are associated with national capital; and whether or not they are monopolistic in their control of a given productive activity. Social and political aspects may be evaluated from the standpoint of a personal ideology, or they may be related to economic aspects and given a politico-economic interpretation. But any approach must recognize that, economically, foreign capital may aid an underdeveloped country, whatever its politics, to accelerate its rate of growth and thereby raise its living standards more rapidly. In fact, such aid generally is essential.

Latin America has received a considerable amount of capital from abroad. It is estimated that in 1913–14, long-term foreign investments came to more than $7 billion,[1] of which one-half was British capital, almost one-fourth was American, and the rest was French and German. By 1929, British and United States capital alone totaled more than $9 billion, with the latter accounting for most of the increase. Since that time, United States capital has predominated, and most of the investments from other countries have been repatriated. But between 1929 and

[1] See Javier Márquez, *Inversiones internacionales en América Latina* (México, Banco de México, 1945), Table I, p. 123.

1947–48, there was apparently no net capital inflow from abroad; in fact, it is very probable that there was a net outflow. Nevertheless, since World War II there has been a renewed inflow of foreign capital, not only in the traditional form of direct investment by foreign enterprises, but in the form of long- and medium-term credits for importing machinery and equipment, granted by official and private foreign banks and by international agencies. It is estimated that in the twelve years from 1947 to 1959 there was a net inflow of both private and public foreign capital to Latin America of about $10 billion, of which nearly $7.5 billion was in the form of direct foreign investments and the rest were mainly official loans, with some private credits. Of the $13.6 billion worth of direct foreign investment in Latin America in 1959, it was calculated that more than $8.2 billion, or 60 per cent, was United States capital,[2] and that this sum represented 28 per cent of United States direct investments all over the world. This high proportion has since declined, while United States investments in Canada and Europe have risen. (See Table 35.)

It is interesting to see how the $8.2 billion of United States direct private investment was distributed in 1959. More than one-third, 36 per cent, entered the petroleum industry, and all but 10 per cent of this went to Venezuela. (See Table 36.) Less than one-fifth, 17 per cent, went into manufacturing, and one-half of this was in Brazil and Mexico, with the rest spread over several countries. The mining and smelting industries, three-quarters of which were located in Chile, Peru, and Mexico, absorbed 15 per cent of United States direct investment in Latin America. Cuba held one-fourth of the 13 per cent invested in public utilities, chiefly elec-

[2] For figures through 1958, see ECLA, *Foreign Private Investments in the Latin American Free-Trade Area. Report of the Consultant Group Jointly Appointed by the Economic Commission for Latin America and the Organization of American States* (United Nations, Department of Economic and Social Affairs, New York, 1961, Publication No. 60.II.G. 5), pp. 9–10; and for 1959 figures, ECLA, *Economic Survey of Latin America, 1960*, mimeographed document E/CN.12/565, Part I, Chap. III, Table III-7. The total value in 1960 and 1961 should be no higher, owing to the Mexican purchase of the electric power companies and the Cuban expropriation of farms and industries.

tric power and transport. The remaining 19 per cent of the total was divided among trade, agriculture, and other activities.

By countries, Venezuela accounted for 34 per cent of direct United States investment, or about $2,808 million, principally in petroleum. Cuba followed with $955 million, or almost 12 per cent, distributed among several activities. Third was Brazil with $839 million, or 10 per cent, of which one-half was in manufacturing. Mexico held $759 million, or 9 per cent, with nearly one-half in manufacturing. Next was Chile with $729 million concentrated in mining and smelting industries. United States capital in Peru's mining industry, Colombia's petroleum industry, and Argentina's industrial activities and public utilities brought the aggregate of the eight countries to roughly 89 per cent of direct United States investment. (See Tables 37 and 38.)

It is estimated that, from 1950 to 1959, the petroleum industry claimed 46 per cent of the increase in United States private investment in Latin America; mining and smelting received 17 per cent; industrial activities, almost another 17 per cent; and other activities, the remaining 20 per cent. (See Table 38.)

By country, 48 per cent of the increase in investment went to Venezuela; 9 per cent to Mexico; 8 per cent to Cuba; 7.5 per cent to Peru; 5 per cent to Colombia; only 5 per cent to Brazil; and another 5 per cent to Chile. (See Table 38.)

The above figures leave no doubt as to the relative importance of United States capital in Venezuela and petroleum, the country and the industrial sector that received almost one-half the increase in the United States direct Latin American investments between 1950 and 1959. Excluding Venezuela, private United States investments in Latin America during that period amounted to only $1,958 million, or a little more than $200 million a year. This sum, divided equally among the nineteen other countries, would give each an annual average of $11 million. Thus, apart from Venezuela, the volume of United States private capital transfers to Latin America since 1950 has been comparatively insignificant, especially since it includes reinvested business earnings. This $200 million a year, or even the $419 million that takes in Venezuela's receipts, are a contrast to the $733 million annual United States investment in Canada, which by 1959 reached an aggregate of $6.6 billion. (See Table 35.) In that year, Canada held 34 per cent of all United States direct investment; Latin America's share had declined to 28 per cent. In Canada, the increase went mainly into petroleum and industrial activities.

The difference between the $7.5 billion total net inflow of private capital to Latin America between 1947 and 1959 and the nearly $5.2 billion represented by United States direct investment can be attributed partly to direct investments from other countries, chiefly England, Germany, Belgium, and Canada, and partly to private credits granted by United States and European institutions. There is no information available on which to base an analysis of the uses assigned to the other $2.3 billion, but presumably some of these resources also went into the Venezuelan petroleum industry. It is calculated that from 1950 to 1956, gross private credits to Latin America averaged $100 million a year, and that in 1957–58, they were $300 million, a portion of which was suppliers' credit guaranteed under the systems prevailing in capital-exporting countries.[3] A substantial share of these funds probably was relatively short term.

It may be estimated that, between 1950 and 1959, foreign governments and international agencies provided about $1,600 million net of repayments,[4] of which $600 million were transferred as grants, some $650 million as net long-term loans from the International Bank for Reconstruction and Development, and almost all the rest as net credits from United States Government agencies, principally the Export-Import Bank.[5] A large share of the capital provided by this bank was to refinance short-term loans for

[3] Report of the ECLA/OAS Consultant Group, p. 9; and Economic and Social Council of the OAS, *Financing of Economic Development in Latin America* (Doc. ES-30-58. Washington, D.C., 1958), Chap. III.

[4] Based on figures in Table 3 of the Report of the ECLA/OAS Consultant Group, and ECLA, *Economic Survey of Latin America 1960*, Part I, Chap. III.

[5] See ECLA, *Economic Survey of Latin America, 1957, 1958,* and *1960.*

imports or for stabilization purposes. Latin America has received from the World Bank and the Eximbank together a net capital inflow of only $150 million a year for development, which is much less than direct private capital annually invested in the region. Nonetheless, the bulk of public external credits has gone into electric power, transport, and industrial production, in accordance with national development programs.

To recapitulate, the total net value of all forms of foreign capital in Latin America in the last ten years has not exceeded $600 million a year. Excluding Venezuela, a net inflow of little more than $350 million per annum went to all the rest of Latin America. Although this is a rough estimate, it gives an idea of the situation.

The business earnings, interest, and royalties on private foreign capital paid by Latin America represent a sum in excess of annual net investment received. In 1947, they reached a total of some $680 million; in 1951, $940 million; and from 1955 to 1959, an annual average of more than $1,200 million a year.[6] Taking into account business earnings reinvested by foreign enterprises, returns on external capital have been even higher. In 1957, United States private capital alone earned a total of $1,096 million, including $239 million of undistributed profits, an increase of 80 per cent over the amount it received in 1950; meanwhile, the value of its investment went up 67 per cent.[7] Of the $1,096 million earned in 1957 by United States concerns, petroleum yielded 58 per cent, manufacturing 12 per cent, mining and smelting 9 per cent, and trade and distribution industries and agriculture most of the remaining 21 per cent. (See Table 39.) Geographically, 62 per cent of this income was earned in Venezuela, 7 per cent in Cuba, 6 per cent in Brazil, 5 per cent in Mexico, and 5 per cent in Panama. It is easy to see the correlation between direct United States investments in Venezuela and petro-

6 *Ibid.*

7 U.S. Department of Commerce, *U.S. Business Investment in Foreign Countries* (Washington, D.C., 1960). Derived from Tables 38 and 46.

leum, and the receipts from the same country and that industrial sector.

By 1959, returns on foreign capital in Latin America had dropped to $774 million, mainly because of the diminished yield of the Venezuelan petroleum industry, which nevertheless accounted for 40 per cent of the total.[8] It is interesting to note that in 1957 remittances from Latin America to United States investment enterprises included $70 million in royalties and fees for technical and administrative services; these payments represent almost 30 per cent of the income received for such services all over the world by United States enterprises having direct foreign investments.[9]

Foreign capital investment in Latin America, therefore, has yielded a substantial return. In 1957, apparently the peak year, United States private capital earnings amounted to 15 per cent of the value of the U.S. investments. By 1959, they had fallen to 9.4 per cent.

In Canada, where United States direct private investment in 1959 was estimated at $10,171 million—24 per cent higher than that reported for Latin America—the average rate of return on that capital was 7.6 per cent in both 1957 and 1959. The petroleum industry in Venezuela and Canada yielded 31.3 and 5.6 per cent, respectively, in 1957, and 14.4 and 3.0 per cent in 1959.[10]

On the other hand, earnings of United States capital, added to those of other countries and to interest on medium- and long-term credits, came in 1957 to 18 per cent of the value of Latin American exports, and in 1959 still accounted for 17 per cent.[11]

Evidently, in recent years United States private investment has yielded proportionately higher earnings in Latin America than, for example, in Canada. Furthermore, these earnings usually have exceeded the net increase in the investments themselves. This has

8 *Ibid.*, Table 37.
9 *Ibid.*, Table 41.
10 *Ibid.*, based on Tables, 5, 37 and 38.
11 Based on data in ECLA, *Economic Survey of Latin America, 1957*, and *1960*.

sometimes led to the rather superficial conclusion that foreign private capital contributes nothing, since it earns more than it annually invests. It has been pointed out, particularly by the United States Department of Commerce,[12] that United States direct investments result in a considerable volume of employment, pay rolls, purchases of materials and services, income-tax revenue, etc. For example, United States concerns in Latin America employed in 1957 almost a million persons: 180,000 in Mexico, 160,000 in Cuba, 140,000 in Brazil, 55,000 in Chile, but only 70,000 in Venezuela.[13] It has been stressed that foreign capital plays a role that cannot be correctly appraised by simply comparing annual investment with annual yields, which generally originate in earlier outlays; and that it can only be evaluated by taking into account its contribution to the country in which it operates. However, from the standpoint of total resources available for economic development, the comparison is valid, because such earnings represent savings generated in Latin America that are transferred to the rest of the world and are not offset by an equivalent transfer of savings from other sources.

A problem of a completely different origin is presented by nationals who seek security abroad for their funds, rather than reinvest them locally and thereby promote economic development. There are no adequate data on flights of capital from Latin America, but currently they could easily amount to $3 billion or $4 billion, amassed over a number of years.

As regards the participation of foreign capital in development, it is necessary first to examine the rate of development and particularly the degree of over-all capital formation in Latin America. Between 1950 and 1958, Latin America is estimated to have invested 16 to 18 per cent of its gross product. (See Table 40.) Although not a very high ratio, it at least indicates an effort

12 U.S. Department of Commerce, *U.S. Investments in the Latin American Economy* (Washington, D.C., 1957).
13 U.S. Department of Commerce, *U.S. Business Investments in Foreign Countries*, Table 34.

sufficient to raise production significantly. But not all countries have made the same effort. In Brazil and Mexico, which account for nearly one-half of Latin America's gross product, annual gross capital formation has not gone beyond 15 per cent. Venezuela and Peru have reported ratios of more than 20 per cent, especially as a result of the increase in foreign investment. In the last ten years, the per capita gross product has grown 1.95 per cent per annum, although in the last five years the rate has been only 1.7 per cent. The above figures suggest that, whatever the contribution of foreign capital to investment in specific activities and countries, Latin America has not used its total available resources, including funds from abroad, to reap the full benefit of that contribution. Thus, there exists a situation similar to the theoretical one described at the beginning of the chapter. On the one hand, Latin America has received foreign capital that has been invested with visible results; on the other, it has employed part of its own resources in unproductive activities, consumer expenditures, and even exports of its capital to more developed countries.

Perhaps the most striking example of Latin America's poor use of funds from abroad is Venezuela, where, as has been seen, the bulk of direct foreign investment is concentrated. Through taxation, Venezuela has managed to absorb 60 per cent of the petroleum companies' annual earnings. As the producing and refining capacity of the petroleum industry expanded, this tax revenue, which at least since 1945 has been appreciable, was supposed to be used to raise the output of other sectors of the country's economy and broaden its productive base. Known as "sowing petroleum" (*sembrar el petróleo*), this policy, even allowing for the difficulties inherent in an attempt to change rapidly the structure of a country's economy, has not been very fruitful. Some of the "seed" was thrown to the winds, some of it was converted into luxury or nonproductive investments, and some of it has generated increases in consumption that can no longer be sustained because slackened foreign investment in petroleum has lowered tax revenues. Perhaps Venezuela should not be considered a representative case, because a country starting out with a backward economy cannot fully exploit investments that exceed the real limits imposed by the labor supply, the adaptability of the social structure, and the organizing skill of the government. In any event, Venezuela's problem is not the amount of resources it derives from foreign investments, but the orientation—for many years inadequate—that it has given its development programs. This problem is repeated, in varying degrees, in other countries.

In brief, the contribution of foreign capital to over-all economic development has to be evaluated within the framework of each country's development activities and other aspects of its economic policy. This is not to imply that utilization of foreign capital has not, in fact, helped expand Latin America's producing capacity. If Latin America is to benefit from the buoyant world demand forecast for certain basic commodities, especially petroleum and mining and smelting products, it certainly will be because, in these fields, foreign-capital investments have enabled the region not only to supply itself[14] but to export. A series of related activities, like the production of petrochemicals and copper manufactures, have grown out of investments in petroleum and mining and smelting, and have signified an important industrial advance for Latin America.

As to foreign investments in manufacturing, they have contributed appreciably to industrial capacity in Mexico and Brazil, where impressive amounts have been committed, thanks in part to the industrialization policies of both countries. Foreign private investment in manufacturing has been accused of a tendency to monopolize whatever branch it enters and to compete with domestic investment on a scale that curtails the possible expansion of domestic enterprise. Furthermore, foreign concerns often have no interest in developing local suppliers, but seek only to establish themselves within a protected market. Such investments are defended on the grounds that they supply the modern techniques

14 See Chapter 10.

resulting from expensive industrial research carried on in other countries; that they provide a considerable volume of employment; and that they train specialized labor. Examples are given of a large variety of local industries that have grown up around the demand created by a foreign enterprise. But no general conclusion can be safely drawn, since no thorough studies have been made of the subject. There are, however, certain strictly economic considerations that arouse misgivings about the benefits to be derived from such investment.[15]

Although medium- and long-term credits from abroad have not been large, they have met the requests of Latin American governments for investment in basic sectors of economic development. Loans have been obtained to increase the output of electric power, to extend the railway grid, to improve ports, to construct highways, to build silos, to establish irrigation systems, and to promote steel, chemical, pulp and paper, and many other essential industries. These loans have responded exactly to the development needs of Latin America and have permitted governments to invest amounts far in excess of available domestic resources. They have also made possible the expansion of public-utility and other important privately held activities.

These forms of foreign-capital participation in Latin America's economic development are subject to the same qualifications as private capital. In the final analysis, they cannot be effective unless a country makes wise use of the aggregate real resources at its disposal. But there is no doubt that long-term credits at least have contributed greatly to raise over-all productivity. Furthermore, they are preferred by many Latin American governments for their interest rates of rarely more than 6 per cent, which do not unduly affect the balance of payments. Such capital imports have aroused some criticism, but chiefly because they have been deemed insufficient. Lesser objections have been raised to the operating policies followed by the international lending agency,

15 The problem of incorporating new technology will be dealt with in Chapter 8.

such as its financing the purchases of only imported materials and equipment for a project, the stipulation of too short a period for repayment, and its attitude toward the promotion of public versus private investment.

There is no agreement in Latin America on which form of external capital is most desirable. Some governments have frankly favored direct foreign investment; more guarded governments have preferred to recommend investment in certain fields or branches of industry, to be carried out in association with local capital. Tax, exchange, labor, and other regulatory measures vary from country to country. But in the principal countries, except Venezuela, the majority opinion, according to a recent report of an advisory group of the ECLA and the OAS, is "rather against than in favor of foreign capital."[16]

Instead, Latin America has consistently advocated an increase in the flow or loans and credits from international and other official financial agencies, and its support of the creation and subsequent activities of the International Bank for Reconstruction and Development is well known. But the United States took the position that foreign capital for Latin America should be mainly in the form of direct private investment. As justification for its policy, the United States argued the primacy of European economic reconstruction, the World Bank's supposed lack of access to international financial markets, and in general, its world political strategy. In brief, the United States was guided by principles completely unrelated to Latin America's economic development, and based on political and ideological prejudices. The first request to the World Bank for substantial funds to be used in Latin America came in 1947, when a loan was sought to expand Brazil's electric-power facilities and increase the capacity of its telephone exchanges. The loan request was favorably received, not because it was essential to Brazil's economic development, but because the applicant was the Brazilian Light and Traction

[16] Report of the Consultant Group ECLA/OAS, p. 18.

Company of Montreal, a private and moreover a foreign company. The Bank negotiated with the company even before it consulted the Brazilian Government, which was to guarantee the credit.[17] Conservative United States views prevailed over all activities of the World Bank and tried to curtail operations of the Export-Import Bank, which had been granting Latin America loans to finance public investment and new industries. The same United States circles opposed creation of a United Nations development agency; instead they advocated establishment of the International Finance Corporation and, a few years later, the International Development Association. Both agencies have been completely dominated by the World Bank.

For a long time, United States opinion also stood in the way of setting up an Inter-American Bank. Finally founded in 1959, it has already aided a wide variety of projects basic to Latin America's development.

The United States Government had earlier put into operation its own Development Loan Fund, which granted low-interest, long-term credits for Latin American projects that were not likely to yield immediate returns. Thus, it was recognized that the World Bank's standards had been too rigid, unrealistic, and in some ways, negative. By failing to support economic development, the International Bank for Reconstruction and Development had not fulfilled one of the purposes for which it had been founded.

Events finally seemed to change the United States attitude toward economic development and the forms to be taken by capital transfers from different sources. The end of the boom in petroleum revealed that, outside of this industry, little private capital was entering Latin America. A price decline in several important primary products weakened the Latin American economy and its ability to finance itself. Also, it became evident that international financial agencies were not progressive. All of these circum-

[17] The author, then a World Bank official, took part in these studies and negotiations.

stances, plus certain negative pressures, stimulated adoption of the Act of Bogotá in 1960, which embodied some of the economic concepts set forth in 1958 by Brazil in its Operation Pan America. It was decided to create an Inter-American Fund for Social Development for financing projects of social significance that would supplement economic development programs, and to lay down a policy of long-term loans for financing the growth of the Latin American economy.

The Alliance for Progress, adopted under the Punta del Este Charter, is an expression of this policy and has ushered in a new phase of foreign capital participation in the economic development of Latin America, based on the principle of larger amounts of credit under more flexible terms and within a framework of sound development programming. This subject will be taken up again in Chapter 11.

5. The Stabilization of Primary Products Prices

IT IS DOUBTFUL that Latin America could accelerate its development without the collaboration of long-term foreign capital. It is certain, however, that development would have been faster in the past, and would encounter fewer difficulties at present, if international market conditions for primary products were less unstable.

Ever since Brazil began storing large quantities of coffee in the 1930's—subsequently using it for fuel, finally dumping it into the ocean, and as late as 1940 burning it, and in these ways disposing of more than 80 million bags of it—the severe imbalance between supply and demand for primary products in international markets has been a principal concern of the Latin American economy. There had been previous disequilibria, especially evident in the cases of Chilean nitrate and Mexican henequen fiber after World War I, but none with such deep repercussions throughout Latin America. Today, besides the unresolved coffee problem, disequilibrium exists in world markets for cotton, sugar, cacao, wool, petroleum, lead and zinc, copper, tin, and other products important to Latin American countries. It should be understood that the market instability of primary products affects not only Latin America but other producing areas as well.

In the past, instability has been defined as "excessive" price fluctuations occurring during relatively short periods, of one to three years, and has been attributed to such causes as government measures, speculation, blights, adverse weather conditions, and finally, changes in inventories. Changes in inventories, which are tied to general business cycles in industrial countries, especially have conditioned the demand for primary products. These fluctuations in demand, confronted by momentarily rigid supplies of world primary production, necessarily gave rise to price fluctuations. Coupled with the cyclical factors were circumstances that affected some products more than others, and the resulting erratic price quotations for wheat, cotton, copper, lead, wool, or cacao had considerable impact on the foreign-exchange reserves of exporting countries. To the extent that a country exported only one or a very few products and derived a large part of its total domestic income from export proceeds, its economy was vulnerable to the vagaries of foreign trade.

Undoubtedly, these fluctuations have been intense and frequent. A United Nations study published in 1952,[1] which analyzed United States import prices between 1922 and 1949 for a large number of products and averaged the annual fluctuations by product and country, showed that, out of 218 prices, only 18 showed a mean annual variation of less than 10 per cent; in 143 cases, it ranged from 10 to 20 per cent; in 50 cases, from 20 to 30 per cent; and in 7 cases, more than 30 per cent. Thus, in most cases, the foreign price of a raw material or a primary foodstuff in a given year could have been 10 to 20 per cent higher or lower than in the previous year. It was noted that 11 products showed still more pronounced fluctuations within a year, and that in certain short periods, movements of even greater intensity were recorded.

Price fluctuations for the majority of primary products important to Latin America fall in the 10 to 20 per cent range. For example, the price of lead oscillated an average of 20 per cent per annum between World Wars I and II, and annually fluctu-

[1] United Nations, *Instability in Export Markets of Under-Developed Countries*, cited in United Nations, *Commodity Trade and Economic Development*, 1953, p. 7.

ated 18 per cent between 1948 and 1957.[2] (See Table 41.) In 1956, the price rose 9 per cent, but in 1957 it fell 18 per cent, and in 1958, another 23 per cent. (See Table 42.) The price of wool varied on an average of 21 per cent per annum between 1920 and 1938, and 17 per cent between 1948 and 1957. In the latter year, it rose 13 per cent, to fall by almost 26 per cent in 1958. Cacao showed a mean annual price fluctuation of 19 per cent between World Wars I and II, as well as in the postwar period. Its price has changed 35 per cent (1955), 43 per cent (1958), and even as much as 55 per cent (1954); pricewise, cacao is certainly one of the most volatile primary products. Before World War II, the prices of zinc, copper, tin, petroleum, cotton, coffee, sugar, bananas, wheat, and meat varied slightly less than those of lead, wool, and cacao. In the postwar period, price fluctuations were less sharp only in the cases of wheat, meat, sugar, bananas, and petroleum. In some years, price changes have been substantially higher than the average. For example, in 1955, copper rose in price 42 per cent, and in 1957 it fell 33 per cent; the world free-market price for sugar went up almost 50 per cent in 1957, to drop 32 per cent in 1958. (See Tables 41 and 42.)

These examples illustrate the phenomenon of price fluctuations for Latin America's primary export products. None of these— not even coffee—are commodities for which Latin America is the sole producing or exporting region. Only three-fourths or less of world coffee imports are presently supplied by Latin American countries. In the cases of wheat, cotton, petroleum, lead, sugar, and others, Latin America does not compete exclusively with underdeveloped and primary producing countries, but contends with industrial countries also. Within Latin America itself, not all countries will want to support the price of a given primary product, because some may be importers of that commodity.

[2] This does not mean that prices moved alternately upward and downward; rather, they averaged that degree of annual change, whether positive or negative. Thus, this calculation may involve cases in which the price fell two or more consecutive years at the rate indicated.

Consequently, the problem of primary price fluctuations is world-wide in scope and does not necessarily imply a clear identification of interests among the exporting countries or among the different countries of a geographic region or a continent. Underdeveloped exporting countries may be in a weak position because there are often far more exporters than importers. When prices fall, importing countries can maneuver to pay even less by acquiring the products from those exporters that cannot resist the temptation to sell more volume at the expense of their competitors. When prices rise, exporting countries may set aside any notion of equilibrium in international trade and try to win markets by increasing production to a level that later cannot be justified. It should also be remembered that world markets for primary products are financed by the purchasing countries, which are therefore in a position to depress prices or at least to prevent their rising.

The above considerations suggest that behind annual or periodic price fluctuations more profound disequilibria are taking shape that cannot be explained merely by cyclical fluctuations of demand in industrial countries or by seasonal or climatic conditions. The disparity in the purchasing power of advanced and backward countries, coupled with the concentration of imports in a few countries and the spreading of exports over many, creates a structural dislocation that tends to lower prices in the long run. Furthermore, the financial weakness of underdeveloped countries induces them to produce and export primary products even in times of depressed prices; and when prices are high, it obliges them to use all their resources for development, which precludes any saving against future slumps. Investments in expanding the production and export of certain primary products do not reach maturity for some time. Frequently, if such investments are stimulated by a prolonged period of high prices, production begins to climb precisely when prices begin to decline, and the increased output creates surpluses that further bring down prices. This is the case with some minerals and with tree crops such as coffee and rubber. It is difficult to exercise short-term control over the biological process of producing agricultural commodities.

Not to be dismissed lightly is the interest of many industrial countries in the existence of world surpluses of primary products, including their own, either as a hedge against inflation or as a reserve in case of war. Should war break out, their concern is first to have ample stocks of raw materials—strategic stockpiles—and second, to have immediate access to available production capacity or to have idle production capacity easily put back into operation. Despite the theoretical threat that in nuclear war there would not be time even to load a ship with minerals, these considerations continue to be important in practice. Because they contribute to an actual or potential excess supply, they have a weakening effect on prices of primary products.

The vast monetary difficulties in international trade during the last thirty years, which can hardly be described as temporary or exceptional, also have tended to intensify the disequilibria in the world supply and demand for primary products. The existence of various monetary zones with different degrees of convertibility had an effect, because it became more attractive to export primary products to the dollar zone rather than to countries with inconvertible or partially convertible currencies. Two consequences of this probably helped to weaken prices: supplies of some products were increased to gain access to the dollar market, and output in restricted currency zones was artificially stimulated by price protection.

Over the years, technical progress has increased world consumption of many mineral products but displaced others. Copper is giving way to bauxite; manufactured nitrogen has almost eliminated potassium nitrate; synthetic fibers are supplanting natural fibers; experiments are under way to produce synthetic coffee. Technical progress also operates in more subtle ways: less raw material is used per unit of industrial product;[3] soluble coffee yields more cups of coffee from a pound of coffee beans; fibers are made more durable; light metals are substituted for heavy metals, or plastics for metals; fuels are raised in heat value; etc. The fact that, in general, income-elasticities of demand for primary products are less than one, is due largely to modern technology.[4]

Another long-term factor depressing primary products is the change that takes place in the structure of demand as the more advanced countries raise their standards of living. The change is particularly evident in the demand for primary foodstuffs, which tends to have a per capita income-elasticity of less than 0.7, and in the cases of oils, vegetables, fish, milk, potatoes, and cereals, one that approaches zero or is even negative.[5] This tendency can be attributed partly to the slow rate of population growth in the more developed countries, but most of all to the saturation of some forms of consumption and the use of increased income for manufactured goods and services. The low living standards and uneven income distribution in less developed countries do not permit a domestic consumption that would offset the lack of demand in the industrial countries. Even if the former could expand their own consumption, they would not, thereby, directly earn foreign exchange. Countries with a higher level of development, determined to protect by various means their own agricultural output, also weaken the prices of agricultural primary products in the world market.

Finally, a part of the imbalance between world supply and demand for many products may be ascribed to the understandable absence of international measures to prevent excessive price increases during periods of violent upward fluctuation, such as the

[3] The cases of Canada and the United States, mentioned in Chapter 2, are typical; see also Table 31.

[4] In the United States, there are, however, exceptions, including natural gas, cobalt, chromite, molybdenum, nickel, aluminum, fluorspar, gypsum, and phosphate. See Fritz, *The Future of Industrial Raw Materials*, Table 1.

[5] See Economic Commission for Europe, *Economic Survey of Europe in 1957*, Chap. V, p. 27; and P. L. Yates, *Food, Land and Manpower in Western Europe* (London: Macmillan, 1960), pp. 91–93.

Korean crisis or the 1954 coffee boom, when low production co-incided with intense demand. The abnormally high prices reached from time to time by certain primary products, largely because of speculative situations, have as adverse an effect on producing countries as do declining prices in other periods. The upsurge in foreign demand has accentuated inflationary trends and induced cost increases in other sectors of the economy. It has also shifted public and private investments toward the external sector, often at the expense of basic domestic market foodstuffs. Furthermore, by generating an exceptionally rapid rise in income, concentrated in a few hands, it has stimulated luxury consumption and investments as well as imports of nonessential goods. Thus, a very sharp increase in export prices may unfavorably affect the structure of domestic supply and, by its impact on the structure of domestic demand, it may weaken the balance-of-payments position. When the emergency or speculative period is over, the fall in prices of primary products can be, and usually has been, just as severe. If world supplies have expanded meanwhile, the tendency to depress external prices is reinforced.

It follows that the instability of export raw materials and food-stuffs is not a problem solely of price fluctuations, excessive or not, to be moderated or offset by some international mechanism, but an even more fundamental problem linked to trends in world development that do not now favor countries exporting such products. A number of factors combine to increase the world supply of primary products out of proportion to the demand trends in industrial countries. This combination of factors can be dealt with only over a very long period of time since, among other reasons, the rate of growth of population in industrial countries is very low. Today, price instability is typically a problem of production surpluses and not of stationary demand: the latter grows, albeit slowly, but international markets for primary products are almost permanently oversupplied. There might be a long-term basic solution if shrinking natural resources and high-cost agriculture compelled industrialized countries to import a much higher percentage of their needs from underdeveloped regions. But, except for two or three important minerals and a few lesser ones, the opposite occurs. Price-support programs and other measures to stimulate agriculture, employed chiefly in the United States, pose a constant threat to the production and export trade of the less developed countries and thus weaken international prices.

What can be done about this problem which, although not new, has become generalized? Some foresight was shown in the 1920's, when, in an attempt to reduce commodity surpluses, international agreements were drawn up to stabilize rubber and tin prices, which especially affected Southeast Asia. In 1930 and subsequently, Brazil dealt on its own with the coffee glut by withholding and destroying its stocks. But total supply was never brought under control because not all producing countries would accept the necessary discipline. Some countries opposed stabilization efforts on the grounds that they resulted in excessively high prices and protected high-cost producers. Currently, world prices, and in part export supplies, are regulated for a few products, including wheat, tin, olive oil, and to some extent, sugar. It has been claimed that the success of these international agreements is only relative; that important producing and consuming countries do not participate; that there are not enough financial resources to accumulate stocks at any given time; and that therefore it would not be advisable to extend these arrangements to coffee, copper and other metals, cotton, cacao, wool, rubber, etc. And there are still a few doctrinaire individuals who oppose any interference with the laws of supply and demand.

In the absence of truly international arrangements, Latin American countries have tried to correct the critical situation of coffee through unofficial but government-supported agreements among producer associations. But there has been neither a complete accord of interests nor unity of action. Coffee-exporting countries in other regions, especially Africa, did not participate at the outset in arrangements to protect prices and, although they have shared in subsequent conversations and in agreements to limit exports, no common front has been presented to the world market. Until recently, the consuming countries, particularly the United States, although collaborating in studies on the matter, did not wish to be associated with any coffee agreement.[6]

The cotton situation, constantly threatened by United States surpluses and by competition from artificial fibers, merely has been the subject of consultations among the countries of the American continent and, more widely, among the latter and other areas of the world. Such discussions at least have made it difficult for the United States to act unilaterally to the detriment of world market prices.

Lead and zinc for the last three or four years have faced the possibility of a price fall even greater than the one they had previously experienced. They are now under study by a group composed of the principal consuming and producing countries. This body has recommended, as a temporary solution to the lead problem, slight restrictions in production and exports.

There are also international study groups for wool, cacao, and other products, and the petroleum-producing countries recently formed a consultative body. Unquestionably, such technical and consultative bodies are useful and necessary. However, they can resolve nothing basic, because they are incomplete and ineffective instruments whose weak measures or moral influence merely can slow down price declines but cannot attack the roots of the problem.

The instability of primary product prices cannot be eliminated by easing its symptoms. It is not enough simply to establish export quotas; to require producer or consumer countries to stock a given product so that sales will become orderly; to fix international guarantee prices without the means to support them. Such actions not only fail to correct the basic problem but may aggra-

---

[6] An International Coffee Agreement, to which the United States and other coffee-importing countries are signatories, was negotiated at the United Nations in 1962 and went into force in July, 1963.

vate it. Moreover, with the fundamental forces continuing to operate, it may be impossible to terminate accessory or temporary causes of fluctuations, because they gradually become part of the underlying phenomena.

If the price instability of basic products is now closely linked to trends in the world economy, to structural changes in the latter, and to the difficulty in adapting primary production to the less dynamic requirements of the world market, then the only way to achieve a relative stabilization of prices over the long run is to promote continuously reciprocal and coordinated adjustments between world exportable output and world demand for primary products.

Because this involves treating the problem of stabilization as part of the world economic development problem, and because civilization today is still far from being able to consider world economic development as a whole, it is essential that the intelligence and good will of nations—especially of their members who participate in international conferences and multilateral consultations and negotiations—be directed at the most obvious manifestations of disequilibrium between exportable production and its prospects, on the one hand, and world demand and its outlook on the other. This approach is being taken by various organizations affiliated with the United Nations, such as the International Commission on Basic Products, several committees and subcommittees of the FAO, study groups on specific products, and other consultative associations. Their activities will necessarily yield results slowly and only in the form of recommendations that will have to be translated into international agreements, and many countries will be reluctant to enter into negotiations that may oblige them, as exporters, to reduce production or, as importers, to persuade their nationals to increase consumption.

Nevertheless, progress has been made in the last thirty years on numerous proposals for international mechanisms to diminish or moderate price fluctuations, or offset their effects for short periods. Most of the proposals[7] contain mechanisms to absorb excesses of supply over demand, or vice versa, allowing a reasonable margin for price changes. These would be applied to individual items or to groups of related products. An international buffer stock would require sufficient financial resources and the continuous participation of the producer and consumer countries representing all or most of world trade in the product or products in question.

One problem involved in a buffer stock is that a base price would have to be set, from which deviations of perhaps 10 per cent would be permitted before the buffer stock would be called into action. There is no reason to suppose, however, that a base year could not be agreed upon and, furthermore, modified in the light of underlying trends.

A buffer stock presents another problem, one that has received less attention: an international price-stabilization fund could not function unless similar national funds were established. At an early stage, the participating governments, both producers and consumers, would have to undertake to moderate international prices by means of national commodity stocks. These initial defensive measures would be taken in the same way that a country combats a threat to the external stability of its currency by using up a safe proportion of the gold and dollar reserves of its central bank, before requesting aid from the International Monetary Fund. National commodity funds would require adequate financing, and regulations governing internal prices, production volume, orderly sales, ways and means of inventory accumulation, etc. All of these unquestionably would present considerable difficulties. National funds would have to be given the authority to correct, as needed, either consumer or producer maladjustments. Otherwise, the maintenance of national buffer stocks would tend in general to stimulate an "excessive" level of exportable production and, in many cases, would intensify inflationary processes.

[7] The main proposals are summarized in United Nations, *Commodity Trade and Economic Development*, Chaps. IV and VI.

Under such circumstances, international price stabilization accompanied by domestic buffer stocks that cannot deal effectively with the problems of disequilibrium, could have consequences, perhaps permanent, similar to those produced by a sudden upward fluctuation.

Those who have studied or recommended the creation of international price-stabilization funds have been somewhat skeptical in their conclusions. This skepticism arises not only from the complications already described, but from the foresight and present knowledge that is needed to achieve a gradual adjustment of world supply to demand. Despite the excellent work being done by various international agencies, this is a difficult feat to achieve. There are three specific cases in which forecasting is difficult or information is necessarily incomplete: primary products affected by substitution of demand originating in new scientific and technological advances; products important as military supplies; and products consumed within the exporting country or produced within the importing country, so that international trade data represent only a small percentage of their total consumption. Coffee is almost the only product that does not fall into one of these categories, and this will hold true only as long as synthetic coffee is not developed. Coffee faces other serious problems, chief of which is Brazil's inability to prevent further expansion of its coffee production, which until now has been unrestricted. Brazil's stocks are one and one-half times the amount that the world market could absorb in a single year, and the world coffee crop in 1962 was greater than ever.

Recently, studies have devised mechanisms to offset the *effects* of price fluctuations, as a means of reducing the instability of exchange earnings in countries exporting primary goods and as an element essential to solving long-run problems of disequilibrium between world supply and demand.[8] Such mechanisms could

[8] See United Nations, *Commodity Trade and Economic Development*, Chap. VII; and United Nations, *International Compensation for Fluctuations in Commodity Trade*, 1961.

exist concurrently with measures designed only to moderate price fluctuations. An international financial fund would offset fluctuations in both price and export volume, and its resources would enable a country to prevent its foreign-exchange earnings from falling to a point endangering monetary stability and development programs. An international compensatory fund or a "development insurance fund," as proposed by a group of U.N. experts,[9] obviously goes further than a price arrangement when it takes into account fluctuations in export volume.

It might be thought that such a function would more properly correspond to the International Monetary Fund, but the authors of the new proposal believe that the Monetary Fund would have to modify drastically its present operating procedures and general policies to handle, with sufficient flexibility and promptness, the type of problems involved in a decline in export value. The proposed fund would function as an insurance fund, similar to social security funds: contributions would not be equal, and benefits would be distributed not according to the amount contributed by the country, but according to the degree of instability affecting an underdeveloped country. Compensations would not be entirely automatic and would require some repayment.

This compensation proposal merits careful consideration. It may be more feasible than previous plans for simple price stabilization, even though it does not exclude the possibility of establishing buffer stocks for specific products, or abrogate existing arrangements, or prevent drawing up new agreements like the recent one on coffee. If it is borne in mind that all these problems are intimately linked to economic development and that the advanced nations are becoming increasingly aware of the difficulties faced by less developed countries, some progress may reasonably be expected in adopting international solutions.

As for Latin America, the latest ideas on the problem of the instability of international markets are expressed in a document prepared by a group of experts for the Punta del Este Confer-

9 *Op. cit.*

ence.[10] After analyzing the current situation and admitting that no stabilization could function if based solely upon the participation of countries of the American continent, they nevertheless recognize that Latin America could take the lead and persuade other countries of the advisability of entering such agreements. Even when they recommend signing agreements on specific products, they point out that on many occasions informal arrangements would be needed to deal with serious and urgent situations. Echoing the conclusions arrived at by the U.N. experts, the Pan-American experts argue that a regional plan of compensatory credits could be developed, and later integrated into an international program like the proposed development insurance fund. The regional plan would begin by providing automatic credits to Latin American countries, to offset part of the declines suffered in their export incomes; these credits would be repaid when exports regained normal levels or after a reasonable period of time. A fund would be set up with contributions from members of the Organization of American States and with capital from the United States, Canada, Western Europe, and other countries in active trade with Latin America. It was also proposed that the countries that increased their exports substantially could make reserve deposits in the inter-American compensation fund. In particular, the group of experts suggested that the Inter-American Economic and Social Council convene a group of governmental financial experts to draft a project for creation of the system they had outlined. These proposals were supported at the Punta del Este Conference, and it was expected that the designated group of experts would present a report before March 31, 1962.[11]

Various plans for coffee advocated drawing up a long-term

---

[10] OAS, *Latin American Export Commodities. Market Problems.* Report of the Group of Experts, Topic III of the Agenda, Special Meeting of the Inter-American Economic and Social Council at the Ministerial Level. Doc. ES-RE-5, Washington, D.C., July, 1961.

[11] The report was taken up at the Inter-American Economic and Social Council Meetings in Mexico, in October, 1962, but nothing positive came of this work.

world agreement to strengthen and more carefully supervise export quotas; instituting measures for stimulating consumption; setting limitations on the planting and production of coffee; sponsoring a study to establish an international fund to ensure a more orderly process of coffee production and distribution. But, even though the approach envisaged at the Punta del Este Conference sought to include the largest possible number of coffee producers and consumers from outside Latin America, it provided no guarantee of international coffee prices.[12] However, international financing was recommended to supplement measures taken by the individual producer countries to restrict coffee planting and production. In this respect, the principal problem is Brazil, where, as in other countries, it is claimed that coffee plantations are too specialized to change over to other crops. However, there are signs even in Brazil that powerful incentives are inducing some regions to abandon coffee in favor of other products, chiefly foodstuffs for domestic consumption and agricultural raw materials.[13]

To conclude this important topic of the stabilization of primary product markets, it is necessary first to bear in mind that continuous instability seriously damages economic development programs because public and private investment plans are interrupted or frustrated by declining external demand. It is imperative, therefore, that Latin America's economic development be assisted by adequate measures to reduce the instability of markets or the effects of such instability, through specific, product-by-product agreements or through inter-American and international arrangements to compensate for exchange losses. These solutions must be considered within the framework of the

[12] Resolution C.1 of the Special Meeting of the Inter-American Economic and Social Council at the Ministerial Level. Punta del Este, August 17, 1961. The International Coffee Agreement signed in 1962 does not guarantee a basic minimum price.

[13] Cf. Onno Van Teutem, "Coffee in Latin America: the Producers' Problem," *Economic Bulletin for Latin America*, IV, No. 1 (March, 1959), especially pp. 38–43.

long-term problems brought about by world economic development, including basic maladjustments between world supply and demand for primary products. Furthermore, no international measures can succeed unless they are supplemented by national policies of development and by adjustments of production to market trends. A detailed study should be made as soon as possible to determine to what extent primary-product instability would be alleviated or reduced by more rapid domestic growth, greater industrialization, and increased regional integration within the Latin American economies. If they stepped up the pace of their industrial development with improved external stability and higher internal consumption of primary products, countries would no longer have to resort in desperation to medium- and long-term credits or to foreign investments as a means of accelerating growth.

6. The So-Called Social Aspects of Economic Development

IF IT IS GRANTED that economic development is not an end in itself but a means to better human relations and well-being, then economic progress must be judged by its social results. Economic development cannot be considered a simple accumulation of productive capacity, nor can the standards of living of a population be measured in terms of steel ingots produced or electric power installed. However, social gains deriving from economic development are difficult to appraise accurately, for several reasons: First, there is no established pattern by which to evaluate them; then, economic development may bring social losses as well as gains; furthermore, by its very nature, development may result in long-term benefits which only become apparent after a period of relative sacrifice; finally, the concept of social progress, of the individual's personal welfare and his relation to society, varies according to ideological and philosophical beliefs.

Some observers argue that, in spite of its many failings and its recently slackened pace, Latin America's economic development in the past ten or fifteen years has produced great social improvement and made possible important advances toward a better future, or in any event, provided a base for such advances. Others are convinced that it has brought few advantages to the Latin American masses, particularly those in the rural section, and that it has created poverty-stricken urban concentrations. Some think that it has left large sectors of the population outside current concepts of welfare and progress, while permitting a small minority to attain a standard of living equal to that found in countries with the highest income. It is said that Latin America's economic development has not been directed toward achieving social objectives long considered fundamental by even the least progressive European countries or the world's most capitalistic country.

Nevertheless, Latin America has formulated lofty social aims, and several of its countries have made considerable social progress. It has been argued that, in some instances, objectives have exceeded a country's economic capacity, and that a shortage of resources, not indifference to social needs, explains why more has not been accomplished. If such is the case, it might be more to the point to speak of the economic aspects of social objectives rather than of the social aspects of economic development.

Although social progress may appear to be simply an objective or end result of development, it has recently been viewed as an indispensable part of the process of economic growth by which living conditions will be improved. It is increasingly evident that the allocation of resources to welfare—education, housing, changes in the system of land tenure, health, social security, better social relations—must be considered an economic investment that raises a country's capacity to develop and accelerate its achievement of social goals. Social and economic investment are today theoretically and materially inseparable.

It is, therefore, surprising that in many parts of Latin America only limited efforts are made to improve or change social conditions and that the supposed urgency of other objectives has relegated social programs to a secondary level. In comparison with other countries in similar circumstances, a small proportion of available resources is allocated to education, housing, the assimilation of marginal population groups, rural improvement, etc. Situations, prejudices, social organizations, ways of life, and collective outlooks persist that contradict the philosophy of progress and human dignity that Latin America has expounded so often and recommends so freely to other regions of the world.

Have the social problems of development been correctly identified? At times, sociologists enter into a maze of abstractions that economists find confusing. Perhaps these abstractions are valid if it is assumed that society is still governed by the automatism implicit in the economic liberalism that guided the development of Western Europe and the United States. But it is difficult to relate these abstractions to the problems of development in Latin America. Theories about motivations and attitudes, and about the rational or irrational behavior of different sectors of society, fall within this category of ideas. These concepts are of little economic interest or urgency. The economist can easily name the social requirements for economic development; but he expects the sociologist and other social scientists to indicate how to surmount the social and institutional obstacles to growth and how to foresee the social consequences of given measures and to provide data and analyses that, added to his own knowledge of the possible economic consequences, will enable him to decide on the best solutions.

The economist believes that the social requirements for economic development include the following: improvement in the quality and extent of education; the individual's adjustment and dedication to a new, impersonal type of work in urban industrial and commercial employment; organization and coordination of groups—cooperatives, associations, teams of technicians, public administration, trade unions, etc.—to undertake jointly certain economic tasks; acceptance and maintenance of higher standards of nutrition, health, and hygiene; training of leadership in business, public administration, trade and professional groups; a change in the concept of property from one of unlimited private use and benefit to a more restricted one recognizing the primacy of collective needs; honest administration of development activities and increased public support for holding government officials responsible for their conduct in office. Progress in these areas —and the economist is not equipped to indicate specific methods for attaining these goals—would help to accelerate economic development under the conditions peculiar to Latin America and, conversely, an increase in productive capacity would facilitate achievement of the objectives of general social welfare.

Education is a case in point. Without overlooking the economic causes of low educational ratios in the majority of Latin American countries, other more deeply rooted, neglected factors exist. According to one authoritative study,[1] in 1950 almost one-half of Latin Americans aged fifteen years or more had never attended school or had dropped out before finishing the first grade; 44 per cent had had some primary instruction; and only 8 per cent had completed primary school. Six per cent had had some secondary or vocational education, 2 per cent had completed or nearly completed these studies, and only 1 per cent had begun or completed any form of higher education. Thus, the great majority had had no educational opportunities, perhaps not even the chance to learn to read and write and do simple arithmetic. Of those few fortunates who reached secondary school, two out of three had dropped out before finishing their studies.

Even though this situation has improved in recent years— notwithstanding the rapid growth of the population—the economist is bound to be skeptical about education in Latin America. He suspects that it is based on erroneous concepts, and that educational programs under which so many children drop out of primary or secondary schools are too long and are ill-suited to the social and economic environment. Since development requires the creation of a labor force capable of learning practical skills in various activities that are certain to expand—agriculture, forestry, mining, manufacturing, etc.—as well as the formation of a professional and intellectual elite, should not systems of early selection be adopted? Under such systems, a high proportion of children could early be directed toward vocational training in

[1] Oscar Vera, "The Position of Education in Latin America, Including a Discussion of Educational Requirements in the Region," in UNESCO, *Social Aspects of Economic Development in Latin America* (ed. by Egbert de Vries and José Medina Echavarría), Vol. I (Paris, 1962).

agriculture or industry, and education could be programmed, scheduled, and geographically located in a way that would take into consideration the pupil's economic and social background. In view of the high rate of drop-outs among pupils obliged to assume economic responsibilities early, would not shorter, less ambitious school programs be preferable? Should not more emphasis be placed on preparing the student for work than on educating him for high cultural achievements? The economist knows that, to accelerate economic development, not only must investment be made in capital goods and the labor force increased in size, but the level of competence of the labor force must be raised continually. An educational system designed primarily to train men for the liberal and technical professions cannot possibly promote steady increases in productivity. More schools and more—and especially better—teachers are not the sole requirements.[2] Education must be oriented so that it will be instrumental in the rapid attainment of economic goals, which, in turn, will bring cultural and educational opportunities within reach of an increasing proportion of the population.

This approach makes it clear that education is an economic problem, although it is usually presented as a social one. Education and economic development must be dealt with jointly; otherwise, there is only a tenuous and indirect link between the two. If education is to be treated as a high-priority productive investment, those responsible for preparing and promoting economic development programs in Latin America must make allocation of resources to education contingent upon adaptation of the educational systems to the needs of development programs. It goes without saying that the resources referred to are not simply budgetary or financial, but real.

[2] "Fifty per cent of the primary school teachers and an even higher proportion of secondary and vocational school teachers have no specialized training for their work." OAS, *Planning of Economic and Social Development in Latin America*, Report of the Group of Experts, Topic I of the Agenda, Special Meeting of the Inter-American Economic and Social Council at the Ministerial Level. Doc. ES-RE-4, June 15, 1961.

Similar situations exist in nutrition and health. The economist cannot object to better nutrition or a steady improvement in health and sanitation, which includes everything from disease prevention to construction of adequate individual and collective housing. Obviously, any program of nutrition, sanitation, or housing has various economic aspects, some of which may be limiting factors. But the economic value of this kind of social progress must not be underestimated, and the resources allocated to these ends should be regarded as productive investments, just as in the case of educational programs. From the standpoint of economic development, the problem is that social programs of this type, which are also educational, are not always properly adjusted to the economic realities of the countries, regions, or zones in which they are carried out. Ideal goals of great social value are established, but they may contribute very little to the economic development without which they cannot be financed, and they may actually hamper growth.

It is possible to illustrate the above with a few striking examples. For various reasons, in almost all of Latin America, there is a very large and increasing housing deficit, particularly in urban centers. It is estimated that 30 to 40 per cent of the population of the principal cities live in hovels or overcrowded slums and that the housing shortage increases annually by one million units.[3] Many of the technical solutions offered are predicated exclusively on construction of new housing and establishment of standards several times superior to present ones. Such solutions are doomed to failure in any underdeveloped country that must invest simultaneously in education, in other social programs, and in increasing its over-all economic capacity. From the economic standpoint, it would be far better to design and execute vast programs simply to improve existing housing by introducing minimum sanitary facilities with the help of the present occupants, rather than to yield to the tempting alternative of razing

3 *Ibid.*

entire areas in order to build great, low-rent apartment blocks that can satisfy only a small proportion of the needs. This is a strictly economic statement of the problem, and it does not indicate any lack of social feelings on the part of the economist. If Latin American countries had a greater immediate potential, they could permit themselves higher goals in housing and build the most elaborate projects drawn up by city planners. But meanwhile, Latin America should resign itself to more modest aims, secure in the knowledge that any slight improvement in existing housing conditions will result in increased productivity and general economic benefits.

Most Latin American countries do not have an adequately developed economic concept of public-health programs. In spite of the humanitarian aspects of, say, the antimalaria campaigns, it is hard to believe that the resources spent in these campaigns could not have contributed more to economic development if they had been used to expedite the introduction of drinking-water supplies,[4] which would have had far-reaching effects on health, or to construct clean market places. Clearly, as long as there exist poverty, poor health, and the conditions favoring them, these grave social problems will have a negative effect upon economic development. However, as in education, the ideal technical solutions are not necessarily best suited to facilitate important gains in economic capacity.

Latin American industrialization must advance rapidly to make possible the attainment of higher living standards within a short span of time. The economist foresees that a social obstacle to industrialization will be the excessive individualism characteristic of both laborer and entrepreneur. Although collective discipline may seem neither desirable nor pleasant from other points

[4] It is estimated that 23 million urban and 86 million rural inhabitants—more than half the total population—live without potable water. Between 1950 and 1960, this service was brought to 21 million people, but the population meanwhile increased by 30 million. See OAS, *Planning of Economic and Social Development in Latin America, op. cit.*

of view, industrialization requires large groupings of workers willing to accept it. As Medina Echavarría says, the industrial worker must adapt "to the social and psychological conditions imposed by modern industry in its three special dimensions—space, time and hierarchy."[5] Latin American industrial growth cannot be based on small workshops or artisans. There is really no inherent or intrinsic reason why the required adaptation cannot be made,[6] but technical training and workers' education programs must orient the outlook of labor as well as teach it skills. Although this is a matter for the sociologist, he must bear in mind the needs of economic development.

Very similar problems are encountered in organizing cooperative action in both private and public economic undertakings. In view of the backwardness of agriculture in a large part of Latin America and the unfavorable conditions that frequently exist in foreign markets and in domestic distribution, there is an urgent need for cooperative or producer organizations in agriculture. The Achilles' heel of economic development is the inelasticity of food production. In many cases, larger investments in agricultural development will be fruitless unless such organizations are established. The economist is not convinced that adequate measures have been taken to organize agriculture, even though there are exceptions. The absence of a spirit of cooperation is a serious impediment to progress in other important activities, including public administration. As long as these conditions persist, uncorrected by techniques and methods that sociologists could provide, economic development will of necessity be slower and more costly.

The era of the Schumpeterian innovator has passed for Latin America. Economic development can no longer be left to the impulses of the entrepreneur, the public official, or the empirical

[5] José Medina Echavarría, "Relationships Between Social and Economic Institutions. A Theoretical Model Applicable to Latin America," *Economic Bulletin for Latin America*, VI, No. 1 (March, 1961), 34.

[6] *Ibid.*, p. 34.

politician. It must be fully recognized that growth cannot be accelerated unless the educational system and the existing social organizations—trade unions, producer associations, public agencies, and others—train in both the private and the public sectors the professional managerial elements who will assume responsibility and make the decisions necessary for economic progress. To date, the type of leadership that has predominated in most Latin American countries is the political or accidental type of entrepreneur, whose fortune depends on the government in power. However, the professional entrepreneur is beginning to appear, along with the "public manager."[7] These same comments might be made about the labor leader. The social task is to create professional leadership for those activities that are expected to expand most rapidly or to take priority, from the standpoint of economic development prospects.

There are other important social aspects of economic development that cannot be gone into here. However, the matter of property has transcended the purely social and economic domains and become the subject of the great political controversies of our time. At the risk of stirring up a commotion among philosophers and jurists and, to a much lesser extent, sociologists, the economist cannot help concluding that the Latin American concept of property is far from conducive to accelerated economic development. The few instances in which private property is subordinate to social or community welfare only confirm the need for Latin America to replace its traditional concept of property with one that will free the forces of progress for its people. The concentration of private property, particularly agrarian, its improper use or nonuse in economic activity, and the resultant social and economic consequences are important obstacles to Latin American development. This situation exists not only in agriculture but also in the control of natural resources, urban zones, and industrial and commercial property.

[7] Medina Echavarría, *op. cit.*, p. 34.

The realities of the land-tenure structure are disturbing to anyone concerned with economic development. Latifundia are still common in Latin America. It has been estimated that, in 1950, agricultural enterprises of more than 1,000 hectares comprised only 1.5 per cent of the total number of farms, but held 65 per cent of the land area. At the opposite extreme, farms of no more than 20 hectares made up 73 per cent of the total number, but occupied barely 3.7 per cent of the land.[8] This is the situation, even with the results of the Mexican agrarian reform included in the over-all figures. Since 1950, basic land reform has been carried out only in Bolivia and Cuba, although it has had limited application in Venezuela and very recently has been undertaken in Colombia. In Guatemala, 0.51 per cent of the total number of farms control 41 per cent of the agricultural land; in Ecuador, 0.17 per cent of the farm units own 37 per cent of the land. In Venezuela, until 1959, 1.69 per cent of the agricultural properties held 74 per cent of the farm land. In Brazil, 1.6 per cent of the landholders control one-third of the agricultural area. In Bolivia, before 1953, 6 per cent of the agricultural properties held 92 per cent of the land. In Cuba, before the agrarian reform, 0.5 per cent of the agricultural units controlled 36 per cent of the area, according to 1946 figures, and the sugar plantations, which owned half of the country's arable land, controlled an additional 25 per cent through rental arrangements.[9] In Chile, 1.5 per cent of the agricultural properties control 75 per cent of the farm area.[10] Similarly extreme situations still exist in Peru,[11] El Salvador, and other countries.

From an economic standpoint, such heavy concentrations of

[8] Thomas F. Carroll, "The Land Reform Issue in Latin America," *Latin American Issues: Essays and Comments*, p. 165.

[9] *Ibid.*, pp. 163, 177, 181, for figures cited on above-mentioned countries.

[10] Daniel Bitrán, "Rasgos estructurales de la economía chilena y su desarrollo reciente," *Ciencias Políticas y Sociales* (México), VI, No. 19 (January–March, 1960), 81.

[11] Edmundo Flores, "El problema agrario del Peru," *El Trimestre Económico* (México), XVII, No. 3 (July–September, 1950).

agrarian property have the following consequences: enormous expanses of land are not available for cultivation; the introduction of modern techniques is delayed; the purchasing power of the peasants remains low; desirable relocations of rural population are prevented; and, in general, agricultural production lacks flexibility. From a social and political standpoint, agrarian reform is now so obviously a necessity that there are few places in the world where it is still questioned. Recently, a greater awareness of its economic advantages has developed in Latin America, and several countries have undertaken programs to reform landholding systems and abolish latifundia. But until more vigorous measures are adopted, in combination with cooperative or community organizations for production, economic development will not receive the support it needs from the agricultural sector.

The issue presented here is more general in character. Because of the scarcity of resources in Latin America, the unrestrained exercise of the right to accumulate private property cannot lead to optimal results; the use made of this property—if any use is made—may interfere with the needs of development. Sooner or later, the concept of property will have to be revised, not only with respect to land tenure and to restrictions imposed in the public interest in urban zones, but more generally.

An attempt may now be made to draw some tentative conclusions. The economist is able to isolate certain problems or important social obstacles to economic development, but he is not qualified to make specific recommendations to remedy these matters. On the other hand, the specialists who approach the social problems in Latin America should familiarize themselves with the problems of economic development, because social measures may solve or alleviate social problems only to the extent that they contribute to economic development. Conversely, it is now evident that economic development is only viable if substantial resources are allocated to relieving social tensions. The real cost of improving social conditions may be disproportionately high, as in agrarian reform or housing programs. Therefore, in countries where the standard of living and economic capacity are barely average, sociologists and other specialists will be obliged to give any social program they formulate a well-defined, functional character. The social aspects of economic development and the economic aspects of social development must blend together into a single drive toward progress.

7. Institutional and Political Requirements

JUST AS THE economic development of Latin America is profoundly influenced by the ways in which the social structure is transformed, so it is firmly linked to political evolution and institutions. Human welfare implies a considerable degree of personal liberty, in all its meanings, but that welfare may have to be achieved with economic measures that require the acceptance of restrictions on liberty, restrictions that vary in intensity in direct proportion to the degree of economic poverty in the community. The problem is whether such restrictions will be accepted voluntarily, that is, by popular consent, or whether they will be imposed by those in charge of economic and social development, even against the will of the people.

Three propositions are involved: First, that economic development can be accelerated only through governmental intervention, which must be more pervasive and active than that of a highly developed country to achieve welfare; second, that unless governmental institutions and instruments are modified or, if necessary, discarded or replaced, they will not effectively accelerate growth and the goals of development will remain simple declarations of intentions; third, that the adoption of new institutional and political forms will have different economic and social consequences, depending on whether these forms are adopted by democratic means and represent the popular will; and, conversely, that the success or failure of economic programs will decisively influence the course of political evolution.

This study of the Latin American economy has stressed the region's low standard of living, which cannot be raised without encountering a number of serious structural defects. These defects are partly socio-economic and partly the result of natural resources. They also derive from Latin America's situation within the world economy and from the latter's development trends. Foreign capital has not entered Latin America in forms that would most benefit it. The price instability of primary products, resulting from maladjustments between world supply and demand, weakens the incentive to growth. The very process of development, which involves a continuous change in the structure of demand, not matched by as swift or steady a change in the structure of supply, creates within itself conditions that easily can lead to inflation and impede growth. The causes of social rigidity, discussed in the preceding chapter, are deeply rooted and cumulative. They make it impossible for the Latin American economy to develop spontaneously, much less at the accelerated rate demanded by population forecasts. Although economic liberalism still has many devoted adherents, the free play of economic and social forces, which in any case has never existed in a pure form, would only aggravate structural imbalances, retard the adaptation of the Latin American economy to world economic trends and convert it into a servile adjunct of the latter, and build up social tensions that could not be pacified. If the "invisible hand" of Adam Smith ever was valid, it is completely inapplicable to present conditions in Latin America and other underdeveloped regions, which need a government's firm guidance.

Actually, the world has been taking this direction for more than a century; governments have intervened particularly in newly developed areas, where they have opened up roads and provided other basic services; they have instituted regulations that have been generally accepted; they have adopted measures to counteract the effect of the business cycle and to avert fluctuations, which today are taken for granted in all highly developed countries. Why, then, is the system of liberal economics still invoked in discussions of economic development? What light does it throw on any effort to solve the problems of economic development?

To accelerate growth in Latin America, social and productive flexibility must be increased, better use must be made of scanty savings, foreign capital must not be absorbed by the economy unless it makes a positive contribution, and this must be assured by carefully planning national investment and the allocation of total resources. To make the most of the varying trends of the world economy, export possibilities must be judiciously appraised. Industrialization, the principal instrument of change in the internal structure, is not possible without incentives and aids to overcome the economic obstacles it faces in Latin America. The government cannot be passive but must take both direct and indirect action to promote, direct, and regulate. Today a policy of development means a policy of government intervention aimed at putting into motion the social and economic forces that, properly adjusted, may produce a swift rise in the standard of living. In this process, the government plays a paramount role.

Although Latin America has recognized that it must have a development policy, just as advanced countries have accepted the necessity of a policy to even out business cycles, it has not yet acknowledged the political consequences of such a policy. Because of the strong liberal tradition in Latin America, many government measures to encourage development or counteract short-term fluctuations are thought of as temporary, as though there were—or ever had been—a normal situation to return to. Actually, economic development does not offer any normal situation and is constantly subject to the unexpected, even if it is patterned after some existing model. It is a ceaseless battle, which can be seriously set back by the least negligence in maintaining defenses, marshaling forces, or planning strategy.

In addition, government measures to regulate and promote the economy are often assumed to be temporary owing to the many blind prejudices and misconceptions that confuse understanding of the scope of "government intervention." As promoter of economic development, the government first draws up a general outline of the nation's future growth and evaluates the possibilities of achieving specific goals through different means; second, corrects any tendencies by the private sector to diverge from these goals in a way that would weaken the over-all program; third, induces the private sector to follow a course consistent with the national objective. Because development is related to changes in structure, the government cannot direct the economy unless it is empowered to intervene, not only globally but by sectors, in the principal variables of the economic system: the components of demand—consumption, investment, exports; and those of supply—production and imports. It also should have the authority to channel private savings into investment areas that further growth, and to divert savings from unproductive investments. In short, the government should have complete control over the allocation of financial resources, both domestic and foreign. To the extent that the private sector does not respond to the positive incentives offered it, or insists on carrying on activities that do not contribute to the national objective or do not provide for the country's needs, the government should effect the essential investments, either directly or through instruments that it can direct and manage.

The amount of government intervention needed to accelerate economic development in Latin America comprises an over-all outline of goals and means: control over financial resources, which assumes an effective monetary and fiscal policy; separate programs for important economic activities; regional programs; the power to stimulate or check, as it deems advisable, the projects of the private sectors. This does not mean that the government has to closely supervise each and every activity of private business and consumers. Once its general goals and programs are accepted and machinery is established to revise those programs constantly and evaluate their results, the government may dispense with a substantial part of the regulations and individual authorizations that it currently follows in many countries to avoid the consequences of irresponsible individualism. A development policy does not require that every investment and every purchase of a raw material be centrally authorized any more than the monetary and credit policy of a central bank requires that loan applications be investigated and decided upon one by one. But an ineffective and deficient central bank policy can no more be justified than a government policy that is not efficiently implemented to accelerate economic development.

Actually, to pursue economic liberalism would be to disclaim all responsibility for economic development and the attainment of social welfare. There are those who choose to do nothing, on the pretext that any governmental action restricts freedom, rather than to look deliberately and rationally for roads to progress. Latin Americans who refuse to accept government direction of economic development are actually shirking their prime social and moral responsibilities, unless they can demonstrate that, contrary to all the evidence of Latin American history, a drifting economy is viable and productive.

Therefore, the major political principle of economic development is the acceptance of functional restrictions on freedom of action in the economic sphere. These restrictions must be accepted voluntarily, and personal liberties must be jealously safeguarded against any encroachment by an authoritarian government. Such a government ultimately destroys the initiative and resourcefulness of a people, especially if, like the Latin Americans, they have been nurtured on a tradition of individualism. Furthermore, it must progressively increase the radius of its influence until it absorbs all the elements that contribute to economic development—that is, until it dominates or nationalizes all activities and curtails personal freedom.

To preserve its ideal of liberty, Latin America must, at the same time that it accelerates economic development, work even harder to progress politically. Since they are mutually complementary, political development should be planned as carefully as economic development, which requires the reform of many government institutions and methods. Sooner or later, some smaller Latin American countries will have to relinquish their concept of national statehood and, through cooperation or more absolute means, merge into a broader economic and perhaps political community.

As political progress is achieved, it should leave behind the stage known as "pluralist democracy," in which the government plays the passive role of arbiter for the various claims of conflicting groups and interests.[1] A government that is not truly popular lacks machinery to give effective expression to public opinion and has to resort to a rather negative system of democracy based on its own interpretation of fundamental policy questions, which may easily prevent it from moving ahead to solve the problems of economic development. This occurs in many Latin American countries. Political progress means that power cannot remain in the hands of, or subject to the veto of, minority groups not identified with the requirements of the national economy. Power must be increasingly transferred to the majority, which shall have its opinion respected and be guaranteed free expression in the press and other media of communication, as well as in the forum of its popularly elected representatives.

As long as the people are not really represented by their government, or do not have a voice in it, or lack freedom of expression, it will be very difficult to accelerate economic development. In such a case, the measures that the government will have to adopt will be opposed by the wealthy oligarchy—possibly entrenched within the government itself—and popular interests will not be properly defended. When there is no communication between government and people, when the electoral machinery does not permit a genuine expression of the popular will, when the people are not educated to exercise their democratic rights, when the government is overcentralized, a program for economic develop-

1 Medina Echavarría, *op. cit.,* p. 37.

ment may fail because of scanty popular support and because of bitter opposition by the vested interests, who want no restrictions placed on the absolute license they have always enjoyed. It is to be feared that, as Cosío Villegas says, in Latin America the idea and purpose of "planned or programmed economic development . . . at present has insufficient or no popular support," and that "there is not a favorable climate in Latin America for a clearly defined program of economic growth."[2]

It is not enough to seek a more representative democracy. Minorities must have their rights protected and their freedom of expression guaranteed. Specifically, the government should be effectively supervised and its policies periodically reviewed to check any abuse of power. Public officials should have to account for their actions publicly and before the legislature. National problems, especially those of economic development and social improvement, should be widely and openly discussed. The government should provide ample information that is both accurate and intelligible. It should encourage and accept criticism. It should solicit more active and responsible participation in political parties, which in turn should devote themselves to studying the problems and plans of economic development and how these are related to political progress.[3]

It is not necessary to wait for economic development to take place before advancing along this course of democratic political evolution. On the contrary, the latter will facilitate economic development and have a positive effect on general productivity.

Institutional reform is another requirement for accelerating economic development. Although development has to follow a central outline that is implemented by a consistent national

[2] Daniel Cosío Villegas, "Política y política económica en la America Latina," *Foro Internacional* (México, El Colegio de México), I, No. 4 (April–June, 1961), 496 and 507.

[3] ". . . the political parties and government leaders of Latin America are not sufficiently enlightened to understand the verity of this idea [programmed economic growth], and espouse it, and make of it the basis of their pronouncements and actions." Cosío Villegas, *op. cit.*, p. 507.

plan covering government action in social as well as economic fields, it is not essential, or even advisable, to centralize execution of this plan. Except for monetary and financial policy, which should be unified and put under a central authority, almost every other aspect of the economic development program can be decentralized either by regional planning or by delegation of functions.

With clearly defined general programs and adequate mechanisms for coordinating them, regional programs will be expedited, local support will be enlisted, and standards of efficiency will be set up that explicitly assign responsibilities. A Latin American country that, because of its size and political organization, lends itself to regional planning, would probably be developed more effectively in this way, but only if relations between central and local authorities are revised considerably so that the latter fully participate in the programs. It is not enough to create regional agencies of the type established to develop some river basin, which are merely branches of the central government. Usually they come into conflict with local authorities, and even with other offices of the central government. Local governments should be consolidated into mixed government agencies that are regional in character, and in which central and local authorities work together under the direction of over-all programs. This is the only way to avoid the system, current in many Latin American countries, of carrying out regional programs that are actually only partial and incomplete aspects of a national plan, when it exists, or isolated efforts frequently unrelated to the basic drive of the region. Obviously, an adequate solution requires a re-examination of constitutional provisions, which in many countries give rise to an illogical and uneconomic division of the government's functions between the central or federal executive and the state or provincial administration. In a national plan to accelerate economic development, there is no room for fictitious sovereignties of local political entities originating in historical circumstances that were not only fortuitous but far removed from considerations of economic programming. On the other hand, a regional and decentralized political formula would give real meaning to the reactivation of the economic and social forces necessary to development.

Public administration throughout Latin America needs to be reformed to make possible more rapid economic development; otherwise its many defects will make it unequal to the demands of future economic growth. One of these defects is functional in nature and lies in its general organization. Under pressure of new responsibilities, the government in Latin America has been unduly dispersing its activity. It has always been easier to create a new department than to reorganize an old one, and to establish an autonomous public agency than to broaden the government's functions. This tendency is shared by other areas, but Latin America cannot afford the luxury of proliferating its public agencies. It implies unnecessary duplication, privileged groups of government officials, and increased difficulties in setting up general standards of administration of personnel, purchases, accounting, etc. Above all, it means a confusion of authority that actually will hamper execution of a unified policy. Each autonomous agency—wrongly characterized in some countries as decentralized—competes with the government in functions and authority.

Almost nowhere in Latin America is this dispersion compensated for by adequate coordination of economic and social undertakings. It is no longer just a question of carrying out through various agencies the government decisions that have been taken collectively by the cabinet or individually by a president acting on the advice of his ministers. In addition, all economic, financial, and social activities of the public sector, including the autonomous agencies and local authorities, must be woven into a general development policy and a program of goals and means. In some countries, progress has been made in coordination, preliminary studies, and programming or planning of development. But the influence of planning and coordination on higher political decisions has not increased noticeably. Nevertheless, again to quote Cosío Villegas, "technicians should not assume sole paternity of a plan for economic growth; they must share it with political judgments, criteria, convictions, and decisions."[4] Coordination and planning will improve when government officials, instead of regarding such procedures as formulas to add elegance to budgets and political programs, become fully convinced of their necessity and cognizant of their mechanisms and consequences.

It has been widely commented that public administration in Latin America is handicapped by excessive centralization of administrative tasks because authority is not delegated. Clearly, this is due to lack of political progress, and to the absence of properly trained administrators and the insecurity of government careers. Centralization is at once geographic, in that decisions on the most minor matters are concentrated in the capital of the country; and vertical, in that, down to the last detail, matters can be administered and authorized only by high-ranking officials or even cabinet members. The actual cost of these procedures to economic and social development can be very great in terms of lost time, discouragement, disorganization, and even money spent by individuals on unnecessary trips. Groups from the private sector of the economy often claim, with some justification, that Latin America's bureaucracy is a stumbling block to its economic development. The administrative system must be thoroughly reorganized, so that authority can be delegated to competent and responsible personnel, provided that their decisions are open to review.

In many Latin American countries, administrative and operative functions need to be separated from analytical and research functions. Too frequently, a person who deals with daily administrative problems must also work on policy problems requiring analytical research. Economic and social questions should be specialized, and their administrative and policy aspects separated.

---

[4] Cosío Villegas, *op. cit.*, p. 510.

If public administrators are guilty of centralizing their authority, overexpanding their bureaucracy, working few hours, and engaging in outside activities, it is because they are poorly trained and low-salaried. There are instances of well-paid, capable government personnel who are secure in their posts and whose skills receive suitable recognition, but they are the exceptions. Not only should personnel be given better training and working conditions, but administrative procedures should be brought up to date with modern equipment, which would also reduce costs. A higher rate of economic development is too vital a matter to be left in the hands of incompetent, irresponsible bureaucrats.

There are other institutions important to the economic and social life of the country that must be reformed to achieve the new objectives. Of these, only the judiciary, universities, and labor unions will be discussed here, although, of course, the press, radio, and many other institutions deserve consideration.

Since the judicial system, in its machinery, methods, and even legal concepts, affects economic life, an effort probably will have to be made to adapt it to the needs of economic development. Many economic reforms, affecting property ownership, taxation, the monetary and banking system, and instruments to regulate investments and other variables, are blocked by the rigidity of legal texts or of their interpretation by jurists. Legal order and stability must be maintained, but at the very least a careful study should be made of relations between the judicial system and the requirements of accelerated economic and social development, as well as of the economic consequences of juridical practice and procedures. Not to be discounted is the corruption encountered at some judicial levels, which necessarily has an unfavorable influence on economic development.

As protectors and promoters of the interests of the working class, unions play an important role in economic development. Obviously, development gains are not going to be evenly distributed simply because the government recommends it. Labor organizations will have to obtain their just share not merely by gaining wage increases, fringe benefits, and other advantages, but by participating fully in all political matters affecting economic growth, including the formulation of development policies. A passive labor movement would be a drag on development; on the other hand, an overly aggressive and demagogic one could threaten its success. Organized labor in Latin America still does not respond to the realities of economic development. Its scope should be broadened considerably, and its leaders should be elected more democratically. Furthermore, its members, bearing in mind that industrialization depends on them, should actively supervise and criticize the execution of development programs as a means of ultimately improving their purchasing power, social situations, and prospects.

The principal shortcoming of Latin American universities is that they are out of touch with the communities they serve. There have been praiseworthy, although somewhat limited, efforts to draw the universities out of academic isolation and integrate them into the activities of economic and social development.[5] Nevertheless, most Latin American universities are not in sufficiently close contact, through their departments and research institutes, with the public and private entities in charge of many of the aspects of economic and social development. Although universities should enjoy absolute intellectual freedom, their curricula and research projects could be oriented toward solving future problems of economic growth and social reconstruction, with the help and advice of those actively engaged in such work.

Although Latin America in many ways can be proud of the evolution of its politics and institutions, they have not yet reached the stage of contributing effectively to more rapid economic development. If important programs of economic development are undertaken, they undoubtedly will generate political and institutional crises. All the current economic difficulties—slow develop-

[5] A good example is the University of Cochabamba, Bolivia. See Arturo Urquidi, *Labor Universitaria, 1946–1951* (Cochabamba, Imprenta Universitaria, 1951).

ment, external fluctuations, inflation, access to foreign capital—have political repercussions, and these are almost always negative. Economic planning cannot benefit a country unless a conscious effort is made to overcome the political and institutional obstacles to development.

8. Foreign Capital and the Transfer of Technology

WITH THE EXCEPTION of the present situation in Cuba, economic development in Latin America has been thought of until now as an undertaking to be shared by government and private business. The degree to which each participates in the ownership of the means of production varies from country to country. In general, the government owns a relatively small proportion of the total productive capital, although in some countries it controls certain industries or plays a significant role in others. The state has taken over some industrial or commercial activities to promote their development or to restrain or prevent private monopolies, but not as part of a gradual move to a socialistic economy.

It is obvious that the government does not have to be either owner or entrepreneur to intervene very extensively in private activities and orient them toward the requirements of economic development. Agriculture is as subject to planning, regulations, and other forms of control in Latin America as it is in other parts of the world, especially the United States. Today, it would be inconceivable to leave agricultural activities to chance and to the free play of supply and demand. Not all farm regulations are justifiable—many of them have held back economic development—but it is a fact that no government is prepared to eliminate them. Changes in land tenure, which are essential to expand production and to raise the income of the rural population, probably will enable Latin American governments to gain considerable control over agricultural life and will increasingly limit the freedom of action and the concentration of holdings of private property owners.

In other areas—transport, mining, petroleum, the generation and distribution of electric energy, some basic branches of industry like insurance and banking—the government is intervening increasingly to direct general policies and channel investments. Private enterprise in Latin America sometimes owes its successful development to government measures that give it much more than simple tariff protection. Industrialization can advance within a general policy of long-term economic development, provided that private enterprise recognizes that in the future the government will assume still greater responsibility not only to protect and occasionally indulge private industrial interests, but to indicate targets and initiate the drawing up of investment programs in which private enterprise and, as the case may be, public agencies will participate.

In brief, Latin America's economic development requires increased governmental intervention and some restrictions on the independence of private enterprise in economic matters, with better results likely to be achieved by persuasion rather than imposition. But this does not mean that the government has to own everything.

How will this tendency affect the present and future investment of foreign private capital in Latin America? And, in general, what will be the attitude of foreign investors toward Latin American development, and what will be Latin America's policy toward foreign capital? Domestic private enterprise may agree to government direction of economic development programs, but can foreign private capital be expected to be as cooperative? These problems have not been sufficiently discussed and they should be investigated. They also demand a definition of the role of foreign private capital in economic development, as a source of both financing and industrial technology.

Of the more than $13 billion of foreign private capital estimated to be invested in Latin America, 60 per cent is from the

United States;[1] and of this, the major part in 1959 was concentrated in the petroleum industry (36 per cent) and the mining and smelting industries (15 per cent), mainly in Venezuela, Chile, and Peru. United States investment in Latin American manufacturing does not represent more than 17 per cent of the capital invested directly in Latin America by the United States, and half of this is located in Brazil and Mexico. The distribution, by activity, of the capital invested in Latin America by other countries probably resembles that of the United States. Private capital has entered Latin America primarily to participate in the development of the primary sources of production, to some extent in public utilities, very little in manufacturing, and only recently in distribution and trade.

The motives for these investments have been rather complex. Natural resources, such as petroleum, have been exploited in Latin America not only for commercial purposes but also to ensure a source of supply that at a given moment could be of vital importance to the United States in operating its economy and maintaining its defenses. Similar considerations underlie mining investments, with perhaps less emphasis on profit expectation, especially since metal prices have weakened in world markets. As for the strategic commodities, the United States is undoubtedly more interested in ensuring their availability than in making profits.

For these reasons, foreign investments in primary minerals have acquired markedly political characteristics, and Latin Americans view them also from a political more than an economic standpoint. Foreign enterprises in Latin America regard government intervention in economic development as a threat not only to their freedom of action as legitimate business concerns, but also to the political and military security of their country of origin. Consequently, such petroleum, mining, and other enterprises mistrust economic development programs and government planning

[1] See Chapter 4.

and inevitably become hostile and even intervene in the country's internal affairs. If in Latin America the conviction grows that foreign capital should not control natural resources, or that investments in the latter at least should be strictly regulated, there remain only the following alternatives: that foreign capital should desist completely from investment in primary production, or that it should agree to a system of participation with national capital and the government itself, that would satisfy the interests of both parties. The choice depends on what position foreign capital will want to assume, in view of the political and economic trends in Latin America, and on whether it will find a more lenient and generous reception in other parts of the world.

The problem transcends relations between foreign enterprises and Latin American governments and public opinion, because petroleum and mining companies and others with international experience have been supported strongly by their respective governments. This explains why for so many years the official United States policy was simply to insist that the preferred method for Latin America to finance its development was by granting facilities to foreign private investment, even though the latter was principally concerned with the petroleum and mining industries. There is no reason to assume that private investment activities have changed basically, despite the recent United States Government policy shift to favor long-term loans for economic and social development. Latin America must bear in mind that foreign investors engaged in the extraction and transformation of primary minerals are fundamentally suspicious of, and even antagonistic to, its plans to accelerate development, and that foreign investors comprise not only the investing enterprises, but also the broad sector of foreign private and official opinion sharing the same point of view.

The foregoing poses a very serious problem for Latin America, for several reasons: First, such investments have been made in many countries and the export of their products is frequently, as in Venezuela, Chile, and Peru, the main source of foreign-exchange earnings; second, because, among Latin American exports, some of the primary minerals, which depend for their market on the industrial countries, have precisely the best prospects for growth; third, the internal development of Latin America requires that the supply of fuels and metals be increased to an unprecedented degree. If foreign investors persist in their attitudes and if, at the same time, Latin American nationalism is intensified, the output of these raw materials will have to be financed more and more by Latin America's own domestic capital. This will divert local funds from other uses in economic development, and will give rise to difficult problems of priority. But even if Latin America gains complete control of its mining and petroleum production, it will need to cope effectively with international competition and to have a guaranteed market for its products in the industrial countries, where most of its output will be consumed (although part will be consumed in Latin America itself). These are some of the many important reasons why it is urgent for Latin America to define its policy on foreign investments, preferably in order to establish equitable systems for both parties to the investment, taking into account all possible alternatives. Of course, foreign enterprises will have to become considerably more enlightened, and public opinion in their countries of origin will have to become more informed about the developmental and other problems confronting Latin America.

Foreign private capital in manufacturing must be considered separately, as the motives for such investments are somewhat different. Fundamentally, subsidiaries of foreign industrial enterprises operate in Latin America not because they consider it a very profitable area of investment—although it usually is—or because consumption in Latin America has enjoyed very brilliant prospects, but because through such operations they thus ensure the market for themselves, forestall possible competition from other countries and local industries, and even reduce their tax burden at home. The Latin American policy of supporting industrialization and fostering new activities has encouraged a sector of foreign investors to immigrate to Latin America and place itself behind the barriers of tariff and exchange protection.

It should be noted that United States industrial investments in Latin America have not created huge factories for manufacturing steel, machinery, or even automobiles, but have established plants to assemble durable goods, to package medicines, and in general to produce current consumer goods. More recent investments have been made in the production of a large number of intermediate products, from chemicals to semimanufactured articles and spare parts. Not all of these investments have been large; many have set up small factories under ownership that is independent of the great trusts and often associated with local capital.

Although foreign investment in Latin America's manufacturing industry is motivated principally by commercial rather than political or strategic considerations, its operation in Latin America has political effects on national development policy. Frequently, foreign investments have been made in sectors of the domestic industry that are socially or politically sensitive, or in industrial branches that have a limited market and are therefore dominated by two or three, or only one, enterprise. This type of investment has striven to persuade Latin America to treat external capital much more liberally. Its efforts have been seconded by a body of foreign and domestic opinion that maintains that Latin America's economic development will be swifter if the doors are opened to foreign private capital. The displacement or absorption of national enterprises by outside ones has caused considerable concern in domestic private business which, with some justification, complains that in general foreign enterprises enjoy financial and other advantages not available to nationals. The monopolistic control of an industry or the simple economic force of the resources represented by foreign investment can easily lead the latter to a kind of interference in the national development policy that, even though discreet or in legitimate protection of its interests, still has serious repercussions.

In spite of the above qualifications, foreign capital in industry is essentially more concerned with the national economy than that in mining or petroleum. Also, it is more likely to accept government economic planning and the conditions necessary for the economic development of the Latin American countries. It shows a more positive attitude and a greater understanding of the national temperament, both private and official. Consequently, private industrial investment can be expected to adjust better to the requirements of accelerated economic development under careful government direction. Presumably, the trend toward mixed investments, in collaboration with local capital, will grow, although the foreign investor may not be convinced of its advisability from a strictly economic standpoint. In brief, the sphere of foreign investors active in industrial production presents less serious problems to Latin America than that exploiting primary products.

Nevertheless, there are important disadvantages to this type of investment. As mentioned previously, foreign investors frequently avail themselves of the Latin American policy of protecting and promoting industrialization to reach quickly a position of dominance in some branches of national industry. In many cases, this is discouraging to local private business. The latter opposes this trend, but on occasion associates with foreign capital so that it can benefit from new industrial techniques. These techniques include not only the specific results of applied scientific research, but also the experience, the "know how," that Latin American enterprises rarely have the opportunity to develop unaided.

Could Latin America's private enterprise gain access to modern industrial technology without associating itself with foreign capital? Could industrial technology be transferred to Latin America on a large scale without necessarily having to go through the medium of foreign enterprise? The answer to this may provide the key to future relations between Latin America and foreign capital in general.

According to three independent studies of the industrial evolution of the United States in the last fifty to eighty years, 90 per cent of the rise in output per man-hour was due to technological advances and only 10 per cent to increase in capital equipment.[2] The rapid technological progress of the last thirty to forty years is largely the result of scientific and technical research, which has multiplied the number of innovations and speeded up the evolution of invention. In 1959, the cost of technological research in the United States was $12 billion, more than double what had been spent six years earlier.[3] In 1960, it was estimated at $14 billion, of which $10.5 billion was spent by private industry (58 per cent financed by government funds) and the rest by universities, institutes, and other organizations.[4] By 1969, technological research is expected to cost an annual total no less than $22 billion.[5]

The technological revolution has been so spectacular—particularly in chemicals and electronics—that many of the most important industries, manufacturers of articles considered indispensable to and typical of present industrial society, have developed in just the last fifteen years, growing 20, 30, and even more than 40 per cent per year.[6] Many European countries, Canada, and Japan have evolved similarly, although on a lesser scale, as much because of their own research as of that by other countries. Nor is there any question that the Soviet Union has made extraordinary advances in technology, especially in recent years.

If economic development in Latin America requires that an increasing amount of modern technology be assimilated to achieve unprecedented gains in productivity, and that Latin America's scarcest resource, capital, be economized, obviously foreign private investors as well as government and private enterprise in Latin America will have to change radically their attitudes to-

[2] R. Solow, S. Fabricant, and B. F. Massell, in articles cited by Leonard S. Silk, *The Research Revolution* (New York, McGraw-Hill, 1960), p. 154.
[3] *Ibid.*, p. 159.
[4] National Science Foundation, *Review of Data on Research and Development*, No. 30, September, 1961, pp. 1–2.
[5] Silk, *op. cit.*, pp. 161–62 and Appendix.
[6] *Ibid.*, pp. 56–58.

ward scientific and technical research. Otherwise, Latin America will be relegated to a state of technological colonialism, wholly dependent for scientific innovations on the subsidiaries of foreign industries.

There are several possibilities of effective action open to Latin America. Certainly, it should encourage the training of scientists and technical researchers, assist its universities and related institutes, and offer to specialized personnel security and working conditions conducive to productive activity. Both government and private industry should strongly support the few existing industrial-research institutes in Latin America, so that they can work systematically and on a scale large enough to yield at least some of the technological secrets now known only to foreign enterprises. Technical progress can no longer be left to the lone scientist, the genius locked up in his little laboratory; modern research demands teamwork and the steady accumulation of experiences and discoveries. Technological research in Latin America cannot advance beyond its present stage of mediocrity unless it receives a massive injection of resources.

There is a great variety of approaches. Research programs can be linked to forecasts of the probable or desirable industrial growth of Latin American countries, or even to development plans. Private enterprise may regard technological research as a means of solving a specific problem, but the government should see in it something more: an instrument with which to penetrate the realm of economic development and to anticipate future needs. These public and private objectives are not incompatible.

An open-minded attitude toward technological research should prevail, leading to the employment of foreign scientists wherever there is a lack of qualified nationals, and to close contact with the scientific and technological circles of other countries. There is no room for narrow nationalism in so great and important a matter, particularly in view of how little effort at research has been made to date.

Also, Latin America should take the utmost advantage of the

very significant body of foreign scientific and technological research that is not the exclusive property of private companies and
is readily accessible to outsiders, because it has been carried on
by a government institute or by one of the nonprofit scientific and
industrial institutions that, for a fee, offer unrestricted use of
their discoveries. For example, the striking advances made in
electronics in the use of semiconductors ("transistors") and other
devices during the last seven years by a leading United States
laboratory[7] are available to anyone who pays a fee and demon-
strates his capability; they are not the monopoly of a foreign corporation.

The foregoing also points up an important aspect of research:
Countries less developed industrially, like the Latin American,
need not carry on original scientific research. They should not
neglect it, of course, but at their present stage of development
they require a large-scale absorption, almost a transplantation,
of discoveries already made in other areas and especially in countries that have recently passed through the stages of development
now experienced by Latin America, and that have put their resources to optimum use. In many cases, the technology of Europe
or Japan, rather than that of the United States, is more adaptable
to conditions in Latin America.

The highly industrialized countries should clearly understand
that they can give a powerful impetus to Latin America's economic development by putting at its disposal, by various means,
an unparalleled amount of technical knowledge. Foreign investments in industry undeniably make available the results of expensive research programs, which are reflected in the constant
appearance of new or improved products.[8] But if Latin America
is limited to the technology it receives through foreign subsidiaries, it will be denied countless technical possibilities, and foreign investment eventually will dominate Latin American industry, in a way that would not be advisable either economically or

[7] Bell Laboratories, New Jersey. See Silk, *op. cit.*, Chap. IV.
[8] Silk, *op. cit.*, pp. 224 and 226.

politically. Therefore, industrial countries should adopt a policy of technological cooperation with Latin America, offering the latter every facility to develop its industry, and enabling its local private enterprise to reach high technological levels and still remain financially independent of foreign private capital.

As long as the notion prevails that inventions and technological advances are strictly private property, and as long as what has been patented and put in the public domain represents only obsolete or even discarded stages of technology, it is not going to be easy to achieve a technological revolution in Latin America. Nor is it at all conceivable that, at this moment, United States private industry is going to hand over magnanimously its technical secrets to business enterprises in other countries. In these circumstances, the practical application and diffusion of many fundamental discoveries of recent years will necessarily remain restricted. Professor Wassily Leontief has said with authority that "such chronic underemployment of technical knowledge might have, in the long run, an even more deleterious effect on the rate of economic growth than idle capital or unemployed labor."[9] Although he was referring to the United States, his statement is even more pertinent to Latin America.

The skillful use of advertising by foreign private capital has not been studied as it should be, but it is still another compelling reason for Latin America to absorb large quantities of technology as quickly as possible. Advertising, circulated through all the communications media, strongly influences the public to prefer the products of the new techniques developed by foreign enterprises and therefore tends to reinforce the position of foreign, versus national, capital. No matter how advertising is judged from other standpoints, and domestic private business uses it just as diligently, it has an unquestionable impact on the ways in which the economy will develop.

Latin America may not be able to reach a satisfactory arrange-

---

[9] Leontief, in his introduction to Silk, *op. cit.*, p. 8.

ment with foreign capital in all activities connected with its accelerated economic progress. The price of close collaboration with foreign capital may be excessive foreign control of natural resources and industrial technology. It is difficult to define the purely economic consequences for Latin America, because they involve both negative and positive aspects, but the political consequences would be entirely unfavorable. However, total rejection of foreign private capital would eliminate many progressive elements, especially in manufacturing, and would sacrifice possibilities of increasing exports to world markets. Pending a dramatic expansion of Latin America's own research, it would also cut off important avenues of technological progress.

But foreign private capital should not arrogate, in technological or other matters, conditions better than those enjoyed by Latin America's private business. Rather, it should share its knowledge, adapt its attitudes to the needs of the countries in which it invests, and cooperate not only in business matters but in the aspirations and programs of national economic development. Until it has learned to accept and participate in the new planning concepts, its role in the national economic life will lead to continuous difficulties, both social and political; until it relinquishes its monopoly of modern technology, it will generate rising resentments.

It is of utmost importance that Latin American governments and private enterprise promptly attack the problem of transferring modern industrial technology to their countries, without necessarily involving direct foreign private investment, and establish some international or inter-American procedure to disseminate "free" foreign technology, seek the release of "restricted" or private technology, and promote and improve applied scientific research in the Latin American countries.

9. The Possibilities of Effectively Programming Economic Growth

IN ANALYZING the problems and prospects of the Latin American economy, preceding chapters have sought to bring out its extreme complexity. Any solution of economic problems must take into account not only the region's economic structure, but also its social and political elements. Moreover, Latin American growth may be benefited or adversely affected by economic trends in the rest of the world.

It has been argued that the economic growth of Latin America cannot be accelerated unless government assumes greater responsibility in the general orientation of activities, the coordination of public and private efforts, and the use made of all available resources. This assumes that government may exert an influence on the variables of the over-all economy and on the corresponding variables of each sector of activity. It does not imply that government necessarily should own all the means of production, although its intervention would be justified in essential or socially significant activities, or in those in which private business does not respond sufficiently to public needs.

If government is to assume these responsibilities to accelerate economic growth, it is evident that objectives must be defined and adequate means chosen to achieve them. On the basis of a very broad plan, government should formulate a body of coordinated measures that, in turn, may be modified to correct deficiencies or divergencies or to obtain better results.

But a "plan" can have different meanings for the economist,

the politician, the enlightened businessman, and the educated specialist. In Latin America, reference is often made to a "policy of economic development," which consists only of a vague hope of raising the standard of living. It is as if an army lacking the necessary strategy and forces were to declare that it had a "policy of defeating the enemy." It is also customary to speak of "government plans" that place heavy emphasis on the investments of the public sector as if their enumeration constituted a program of economic development. This is as if an army sought to win a war by listing the matériel it possessed and intended to acquire. A program of economic development cannot adopt an objective without explaining how it is to be reached, nor can it draw up a list of tools, no matter how carefully they may be set out in order of priority, without indicating objectives. For the economist, whose world is of relative magnitudes and quantitative relationships, a program of economic development has to be expressed in numbers. Objectives and means are empty unless they are stated, or their results may be measured, in magnitudes of clear, even if approximate, economic significance.

Consequently, economic planning must start with a solid statistical base. Minimal information about a country should include its level of income, its demographic and occupational structure, its productive capacity and how much it increases or decreases each year, and its rate of capital replacement. By reconstructing these data, it is possible to establish certain relationships—for example, between increments in investment and in output—that are important guides to the future. An analysis of foreign trade figures and, in general, all information pertaining to growth, or its lack, in the past is useful in programming.

It is no exaggeration to say that ten years ago reliable statistics did not exist in Latin America. Estimates of national product and the components of aggregate demand were just beginning to be made. There were, of course, census data on population, agriculture, industry, etc., but not in all countries. Even today, in more than one country the total population is a very rough figure and the demographic structure is mere conjecture. Agricultural and industrial censuses have been poorly conducted, limited to a few countries, and taken at too long intervals. Moreover, they have not always yielded the kind of information that would be helpful to programming. The occupational distribution of the active population cannot be gauged precisely, even for 1950, when fairly complete data were compiled.[1] Knowledge of the distribution of urban and rural population is handicapped by problems of definition; depending on the country, an urban center can be a minimum of 2,000 inhabitants or as much as 20,000. Foreign trade figures, traditionally the most carefully recorded, are actually full of errors in Latin America, and require complicated and detailed adjustments before they can be correctly interpreted and utilized in programming studies. The remaining components of the balance of payments—and many items are still unknown—have been systematically computed only since 1950. Social statistics, on education, health, housing, etc., are even more incomplete and deficient than economic statistics.

Nevertheless, considerable progress has been made in recent years, thanks to the efforts of international agencies and the growing interest of many governments in improving essential data and in training technical personnel. The Inter-American Statistical Institute and the Statistical Office of the United Nations have assisted in preparing Latin American censuses and in improving many of the more important statistics. United Nations' agencies specializing in such fields as agriculture, labor, and health have also worked to make data more accurate and uniform, and have carried out very useful studies. Unquestionably, the agency that has done most to measure numerically the Latin American economy is the United Nations Economic Commission for Latin America, whose experts not only have ventured to estimate many of the magnitudes not recorded in ordinary statistics, but by their exhaustive reports analyzing and interpreting the

[1] Returns of the 1960 censuses are only now (1963) beginning to be available.

problems of economic development, have stimulated national groups to improve further those analyses and revise basic data.

Sometimes, the worst enemy of economic programming is the statistical specialist with a zeal for mathematical precision. In the absence of reliable basic data, it is entirely legitimate to make estimates. Statisticians can delay programming many years when they insist on a complete groundwork of information. Unfortunately, the amount budgeted for statistical work is notoriously insufficient and the training of technical personnel and the organization of statistical services leave much to be desired. Programming must be initiated without delay, using available information. Nothing is to be gained by postponing it because of incomplete or inexact data. These failings, known beforehand, have to be adjusted for by means of cautious interpretation based on rough estimates. However, economists are eager for governments to allocate adequate funds for organized statistical work, so that future interpretations may involve less guesswork.

The statistical handicap is serious but not fundamental. Most Latin American countries have made substantial progress in overcoming it, because as they have gone deeper into the many aspects of programming, they have uncovered more definite data. In almost all countries, national accounts have been prepared, demonstrating the relationship between the principal economic magnitudes, and in many, investment expenditures have been broken down by sectors of activity, and consumption by categories. In several countries, the structure of demand is known, particularly the distribution of personal income among the social sectors. A more precise idea is being formed of the structure of savings and of the financing of investment. Under the stimulus of the International Monetary Fund, monetary and financial statistics have noticeably improved. Many countries have constructed input-output tables for industry that reveal its structure and how its different branches are interrelated. Methods based on sampling are being set up to estimate agricultural production, which undoubtedly will lead to a greater understanding of why this sector generally falls behind in economic development. Increasingly, the agencies that promote or are in charge of the main investment projects in each activity are provided with more complete, detailed information about the relevant economic phenomena and about consumption and other trends, which they need as guideposts.

Thus, despite its deficiencies—more in some countries than in others—Latin America is technically equipped to carry out a programming of development covering both general macroeconomic aspects and the relationships between sectors.[2] A growing number of Latin American economists and specialists in other branches of the social sciences are being trained and are obtaining experience in programming, and they could do very effective work if their governments recognized that they are at least as important as a military general staff. The war to abolish poverty and advance the economy must be put under the command of an economic general staff made up of the available trained personnel and, later, the future graduates of the many specialized courses today offered in Latin America and in other parts of the world.

Unless Latin American countries learn much more about their physical resources, the programming of economic development will remain a mere academic exercise. In order to set over-all goals and decide on the best ways to reach them, information on the technical possibilities of investment and production must be furnished by engineers, scientists, and other specialists. For example, mineral resources, timber stands, the extent of arable land, fisheries, and estimates of run-off in drainage basins must be studied quantitatively and qualitatively, so that general programs can be treated by sectors. Similarly, the skills of technological researchers and technical experts will be required in every important branch of industry. At this moment, it is difficult to assess

[2] For example, the information presented by the ECLA and the Argentine Government in *El desarrollo económico de la Argentina (Análisis y proyecciones del desarrollo económico, V)* (United Nations, 1959, 5 vols.) is remarkably complete and of great value to programming. (Not available in English.)

the degree of information available to Latin America or the principal Latin American countries. Natural resources have barely begun to be systematically investigated and measured. Past findings by foreign investors have not been made available to the agencies in charge of economic planning. There is still a lack of coordination of private and public efforts to improve knowledge of resources. Surveys, which are usually very expensive, have recently received valuable support from international technical-assistance programs, especially the United Nations Special Fund. As in the matter of statistics, the solution is not to wait for the basic studies to be completed, but to start out with what already exists and incorporate additional information as it comes to light.

Does Latin America organize its economic programming properly? Programming, particularly, requires viewing the economy as a whole and not by isolated parts, whether by activities or segments of demand. Planning or programming of investments by the public sector may be desirable, but it alone does not solve the problems of economic development. A classification of government expenditures and sources of income may be very useful, but it is ineffective unless it includes the rest of the public sector and the impact of that sector on the private economy. It may be worthwhile to attempt the planning of one sector, such as electric power or petroleum, transport or livestock, or a region of the country, but that sector's contribution to the general problems of growth cannot be evaluated unless it is related to the over-all economy.

With few exceptions—notably Colombia, Chile, Ecuador, and Venezuela, and, in its own way, Cuba—Latin American governments have not organized central groups of economists to carry out the preliminary studies for development programming. In several countries, broad analytical studies have been produced by a public agency, such as a ministry, the central bank, or the government development bank, or different partial, and often uncoordinated, studies have been made. Sometimes they have been prepared with the technical collaboration of the ECLA or other international agencies. Many of these studies have been utilized in ten-year projections that, by setting up a goal of real per capita income, permit an estimate of the volume of investment, changes in structure, forms of financing, and general policy that will be necessary. But little of all this has been translated into action. Latin American governments accept, perhaps more than before, the idea of programming development, but they do not execute it, because they are satisfied to follow a development policy that is not defined in terms of targets or quantitative relations and magnitudes.

Obviously, the obstacle is a political one. Almost no Latin American government is willing to entrust to a team of economists the general and sectoral studies that will chart the economic course of the country for the next ten years. Politicians ignorant of the true nature of programming may very well believe that by centralizing it in a group of experts, they are handing over part of their authority and curtailing their freedom of action, in the same way that a patient is obliged to follow his physician's advice. This is a very narrow concept of the political life of a country. Given the kind of problems that today confront Latin America, it is probable that the security of political careers and the permanence of political parties will depend on how carefully development programs are drawn up and how intelligently they are presented to the public and executed. If a country gains from programming, its able politicians are also certain to benefit.

It may be assumed that part of a government's reluctance to entrust a group of experts with development programming arises from its apprehension of a possible conflict between some short-term policy it may be compelled to adopt and the long-term policy recommended by the programming team. A few years ago, a high-ranking Mexican Government official stated: "If the Government followed the advice of the experts and succeeded, everyone would say that its policy depended on their approval, and this is harmful politically; on the other hand, if the Government disregarded the experts and failed, everyone would blame and attack it for not having followed their advice, and this is just as harmful politically." As long as this attitude prevails, programming is doomed, or at best it will be an expensive toy to be used or put aside, according to convenience. For example, it might be employed during an election period and shelved once the new government was installed; or it might be employed to obtain loans from abroad and later discarded as impractical, especially if it involved politically awkward social, tax, agricultural, or monetary measures.

Actually, development programming does not have to pose problems of this type. In the first place, it is essentially non-political. The programming group should be given the objectives, or a principal objective, such as the level of real per capita income to be reached in ten years, and several conditioning objectives, such as better social and regional distribution of income. Once these targets have been specified, the programming group should make the necessary projections to determine the sectoral targets that must form part of the over-all goals, and should indicate the means, for which there may be several alternatives, by which those goals can be attained. In all cases, the final decisions will be taken not by the one who draws up the programs, but by the one who is responsible for their execution. But how much better it is that he should fully understand the reasons for his decisions.

Actually, there is no real conflict between long-term programming of development and short-term economic policy. Programming studies have to proceed slowly, especially at the beginning, and no government can afford to remain idle while its economists complete their research. But this urgency for action is not at variance with programming, which could be executed by stages. Although work would continue on the entire program, the first stage would be a preliminary appraisal of trends and possible goals and how they would incorporate the immediate development policy or the part of the short-term economic policy affecting important aspects of development. Long-term programs would also have to take into account short-term measures already in operation or any other rigid elements deriving from previous policies. And because a long-term policy is made up of many short-term policies, the latter would have to be guided by the former.

Basically, a government may use programming to determine the total investment it will need to achieve higher production and consumption within a given period. The aggregate investment must then be divided among the activities, in each case indicating the proportions to be contributed by government and the private economy, respectively. As a counterpart to an investment program, a financing plan should assign the different forms of domestic savings to the entire programmed investment and estimate, over-all and by sectors, how much will be required in the form of external savings, that is, foreign loans or investments, including those from international agencies.

Because economic development involves a considerable structural change, programming should anticipate changes in the interrelationships of national activities—whether agricultural, industrial, or the services—or in the component branches of each activity. There are two general reasons for defining programming at the level of such activities: first, the tendency for people to emigrate from rural to urban areas and look for employment in commercial and industrial occupations, so that a demand for non-agricultural labor must be continually created; and second, the prospect for a barely moderate growth of external demand, a characteristic of Latin American countries that has already been pointed out. There is little hope of an export trade dynamic enough to offset the increases in imports normally generated by expanding incomes and required by the higher rate of investment. Therefore, Latin America will need deliberately to intensify its policy of replacing imports with domestic production. Replacement should be realized in the agricultural sector and, in fact, in any sector where future demand may be expected to generate imports. It is most urgent in the industrial sector, especially in consumer goods and, increasingly, intermediate products and even some capital goods. Import replacement offers sectoral programming a very fertile field, in which the situation and outlook of demand and production in each branch of industry need to be related not only to general social and political phenomena, but to the outlook, first, of each one of the other branches of industry and, finally, of the rest of the economy.

Latin America already recognizes that industrial programming is essential to accelerated economic development and is giving it careful attention. The problem is how to put programming into practice, once economists and other experts have worked on the problem of interrelationships in a changing economy. It is not possible to program only the industrial branches that are monopolized or dominated by the government, because difficulties in the private sectors, through lack of a program or insufficient growth, can cause government expansion programs to fail. For this reason, the present Latin American trend to consider it sufficient to program the public sector is a mistake. During a first stage, the private sector should also be programmed, at least its most important industries, particularly those, like steel and chemical manufacturing, that are the basis of many others.

How can the private sector be incorporated into the programming of industrial growth? This presents problems connected with the general climate of economic development and with prevailing political conditions. From a purely technical standpoint, there is no doubt that the private and public sectors can agree on goals for industrial branches, the amount of investment required, and the most desirable forms of financing. The private sector would certainly gain a great deal by participating in programming, since in no other way could it see the economy as a whole or appreciate its perspective. This collaboration would enable the public sector to obtain some benefit also, above all if the private sector, by means of some appropriate machinery, were represented by economists trained in programming. In this way, the public sector would hear criticism from private enterprise and would be more aware of the latter's plans and projects. There would undoubtedly be conflicting interests, but there would be still more points of agreement based on mutual interests.

The conflict might be—and at present in many Latin American countries is—of a political cast. In several countries, the private sector accepts no positive government intervention, orientation, or even suggestion, although it has no choice but to abide by negative directives. The private sector is made up of both conservative and progressive businessmen, who are frequently in serious disagreement. It also includes opportunists, who try to induce governments to embark on badly conceived projects that occasionally involve huge amounts of official and even international resources. The private sector almost always distrusts official proposals and regards programming as an attack on free enterprise. In addition, foreign concerns in private business, whose activities are sometimes guided by considerations alien to the economy of their host country, may fiercely resist programming for reasons of principle, because they fear losing their hegemony in industry, or in the case of mining and smelting or petroleum, because their investments are thought of as an adjunct of the economy of the investing country and not as an integral part of the Latin American country.

Clearly, Latin America faces a formidable task of persuasion and education in order to incorporate the private sector into the programming of development. The success of this undertaking will depend largely on the type of men who direct industrial, banking, and commercial activities, and also on the governments which, unless they believe that private enterprise can be dispensed with, should adopt a reasonable attitude combining tolerance and firmness. From the standpoint of government, banking and finance is a sector that must be convinced of the necessity of programming and that must adapt itself to the latter's objectives. Today in Latin America, private banking and financial institutions adjust their activities to the monetary and credit policies laid down by the government to meet short-run problems connected with inflationary trends or the balance-of-payments situation. Because the majority of central banks, or agencies that perform the same functions, have been nationalized, they are in complete accord with official policy. A significant part of the money market in Latin America and a substantial portion of investment resources are channeled by the central bank and official development corporations or institutes toward the needs of economic development. Therefore, a system is beginning to take shape that, duly reinforced, can materially contribute to the financial aspects of development programming and, in turn, have an impact on investment and production. Private enterprise in general will have to realize gradually that a programmed development is the best guarantee of the survival of the mixed public and private economy that currently prevails in Latin America and that seems to respond to the aspirations of the Latin Americans.

In discussing the obstacles to the different aspects of the programming of economic development, this chapter does not propose to discredit it but to appraise it realistically. Nothing would be more dangerous than to expect miracles from programming, as if it were a magic wand to be waved by the economists. Programming is a difficult undertaking in any economic system, even in a socialist economy where there is no conflict between public and private interests and where the people consume exactly what is made available to them by the central planning commission. In a mixed economy like the Latin American, under a political system that is essentially democratic, effective programming is even more difficult. Nevertheless, these problems must be taken up and solved, so that programming can help Latin America realize its hope of a better life.

10. The Integration of the Latin American Economies

IN ANY TREATMENT of Latin America as a group of nations sharing the same economic problems and social aspirations and therefore having basically common interests vis-à-vis the rest of the world, there is a strong temptation to go beyond a discussion of the development of each national economy and consider the Latin American economy as a whole. For historical reasons, for ethnic affinity, for political motives, and for economic convenience, the economic and social development of all Latin America should be viewed as a process of integrating its component nations and abolishing economic, cultural, social, and perhaps someday political frontiers. This, Bolívar's dream, has yet to be fulfilled even on the smaller scale of Morazán's attempted Central American union.

Between dream and reality stand a century and a half of disunion, with each country understandably working to consolidate its own nationality before embarking on a federation of several or all of the countries. At the same time, their economies have developed in different directions, each one oriented separately toward world trade, and linked more closely to the economies of the industrial countries than to those of the other Latin American countries. The movements of trade and foreign investments tended, at least until World War I, to create a Latin American economy—or rather, twenty more or less parallel and disconnected economies—that complemented the European and United States economies.

As long as Latin America produced chiefly foodstuffs and raw materials, the possibilities of integration were determined by differences in climate and the occasional mineral requirements of some nonproducing country. But the trend to industrialization, which began mildly during the first forty years of this century and intensified dramatically after World War II, has opened up entirely new possibilities. Simultaneously, there has been a decline in world demand for Latin America's exportable primary products. This circumstance, coupled with market fluctuations and a deterioration of the terms of trade, as well as the relatively scant capital movement from abroad, has forced import expenditures to be restricted to only the most essential commodities, the others to be replaced by domestic production. Because of poor balance-of-payments prospects, governments have taken measures to stimulate industrial development, which is needed also to absorb the influx of rural population to the cities.

Among the principal obstacles to Latin America's industrial development have been the lack of trained technicians and experienced managers, scarcity and cost of domestic capital, consumer preference for imported articles, inadequacy and high cost of electric power, and inefficiency of other public utilities. Nevertheless, the major roadblock seems to have been, and continues to be, the lack of a sufficiently large market. Latin American countries, owing to the form of their earlier economic development and to their social structure, have seldom provided markets that would enable manufacturing industries to operate at the high level of capacity and the low costs required for successful competition with imported products. Still more important, limited markets have retarded or postponed expansion of existing industries and have prevented establishment of new ones. Some Latin American countries have industrialized within their own economic and political borders to the point where national output satisfies internal demand for manufactured consumer goods, but they are finding it increasingly difficult to go on to the next stage of producing intermediate goods and equipment, which usually requires large-scale output based on a broad market. Other countries with small populations and a low living standard have been hard put to replace imports of the most ordinary consumer goods. In all these situations, the inadequate market can be attributed not only to the country's size but to its social structure, especially its distorted income distribution, and to its economic and occupational structure, which relegates the majority of the population to agricultural pursuits that barely yield a subsistence income. In brief, lack of development is in itself the greatest limitation to Latin America's industrialization.

Therein lies the appeal of free trade among Latin American countries as a means of adding another dimension to their industrial and agricultural development. It would enhance the possibilities of industrial investment and production and would advance projects that otherwise would have to wait many years for a sufficiently large national market.

This has been the idea underlying many of the various attempts to establish economic or customs unions among different groups of Latin American countries, notably those of the River Plate, the agreement for industrial integration negotiated by Argentina and Brazil in 1939, and several free-trade treaties signed between Central American countries. Only recently has there been the thought of creating a large Latin American area for free trade in industrial and other products, to accelerate and reinforce the processes of economic development in each and every one of the countries. This concept supplies a link missing in the earlier proposals for Latin American integration based on simple cultural ties or supposedly analogous political systems or political interests. Because economic development is recognized today as a highly important, if not the most important, problem in Latin America, it is both logical and desirable to try once again to realize the dream of integration, this time as an instrument of development.

In view of the pattern of economic development in the past, very little trade between the Latin American countries could be expected in primary products, much less in manufactured articles handicapped by high costs and customs barriers that were sometimes more unfavorable to Latin American than to United States, European, or Japanese products. Transportation difficulties, the lack of credit facilities, numerous monetary obstacles, and in general, ignorance of one another's economies have also inhibited trade in Latin America. At present, only about 10 per cent of Latin America's trade is carried on within the region, and this is mainly limited to the southern countries, especially Argentina, Brazil, Chile, Peru, Uruguay, Bolivia, and Paraguay as importers of Latin American goods, and Argentina, Brazil, Chile, Peru, and Venezuela as exporters to the rest of Latin America. These countries absorb more than four-fifths of intra-Latin American trade. Foodstuffs, mainly wheat, wheat flour, coffee, and fresh fruit (bananas), account for more than half of this trade, fuels for nearly a fourth, and various raw materials, chiefly lumber and cotton, for the remainder. Until very recently, manufactured goods comprised only 3 per cent of intra-Latin American trade, but now they are beginning to assume increasing importance.

These trade characteristics have raised many doubts about the possibility of creating a great Latin American market. The most frequently expressed is that industrial production in the component countries is parallel and that high-cost industries, some of them excessively protected and manufacturing expensive, inferior products, cannot afford to enter free trade and thus be exposed to ruinous competition. But this is an erroneous argument. Industrial production is not parallel. Even though some countries have reached similar stages and developed the same general manufacturing branches, the structures are diversified and different kinds and qualities of articles are produced. Furthermore, a dynamic concept of the industrialization process is required. If demand for finished manufactures and intermediate goods has failed to stimulate any local output or if it outstrips a country's industrial capacity, it could be met by the surplus of another Latin American country rather than by imports from abroad. Conversely, if domestic consumption cannot support the minimum production needed to set up or enlarge a factory, intra-Latin American trade can provide a bridge to the next stage of industrial growth.

The integration of Latin American industrial markets offers, therefore, ample opportunities for existing industries to increase their trade in manufactured goods. But it is in fact aimed principally at developing industrial activities that must operate on a very large scale; these cover the broad range of iron and steel processing and engineering industries, metal products and domestic appliances, and automobile and machinery manufacturing, all of which are barely beginning to be developed in Latin America. These activities must be entered into not only because they represent a logical succession of stages in industrial development, but because exports of goods and services to the rest of the world will not be sufficient—even assuming more intensive use of foreign loans—to pay for the volume of imported machinery and intermediate products that will be demanded by a constant increase in internal investment. And unless Latin America's productivity and output capacity are expanded through internal investment, the increase in real income will not keep up with population growth, which means it will not be possible to raise appreciably the per capita income level and, in turn, the living standard.

Thus, integration of the Latin American economies is just as indispensable to the policy of development as are the purely internal requirements. Besides opening up new possibilities of commodity trade and broadening the industrial base, it may be expected to help introduce improved technical methods and amortize the cost of the technical research referred to in Chapter 8. A free-trade area would give private enterprise greater incentive to invest, coordinate its efforts, and extend the scope of its ideas and methods. As a natural outlet for primary-product surpluses that cannot be sold in the world market, it would reduce price instability. Public investments with long amortization periods would be more fully utilized, especially in sectors such as transportation. In brief, integration would expedite economic development.

So far, Latin America has taken very limited but realistic steps toward economic integration. Elimination of all tariff barriers, although an ideal solution, has not been attempted even in Europe, with its greater economic capacity and its remarkable progress in industry and agriculture since World War II. Latin America considers the common market a distant goal, to be approached through a gradual liberalizing of trade. This would be accomplished by annual negotiations that over twelve years would progressively create a substantial intra-Latin American trade in commodities largely free of duties, charges, and other restrictions. The countries of the free-trade area would be permitted to maintain their own external customs tariffs vis-à-vis the rest of the world and to accelerate trade liberalization whenever advantageous.

The ideas sketched above culminated in the Latin American Free-Trade Association established in Montevideo in February, 1960, by seven countries: Argentina, Brazil, Chile, Mexico, Paraguay, Peru, and Uruguay. When the Montevideo Treaty went into force in June, 1961, Bolivia, which had participated in the earlier negotiations, decided to postpone its adherence; however, it was announced that Colombia and Ecuador would subscribe to the free-trade area[1] and that Venezuela would continue to examine the possibility of entrance. Except for Venezuela, the free-trade area includes all the countries in Latin America that have reached a relatively high level of industrial development.

There has always been a stronger desire for union in Central America than in Latin America as a whole. In 1952, the five Central American countries, aided by the ECLA and other United Nations agencies, undertook a long series of studies designed to promote a close integration of their economies based

[1] Colombia and Ecuador joined the LAFTA at the end of 1961.

on free trade, industrial specialization, and coordination of their economic development programs. Integration is even more justified in so fragmented a region, as no Central American country alone could easily effect the structural changes and, above all, achieve the industrial development necessary to raise appreciably the standard of living. The political immaturity and narrow attitudes of some sectors of the Central American population, however, have prevented the completion of many of these projects, even those involving only simple cooperation in matters of mutual interest or standardizing important economic legislation. After many vicissitudes and a considerable number of treaties that were signed, ratified, but never implemented, the goal of a common market in Central America was reduced by 1960 to an agreement among four countries: El Salvador, Guatemala, Honduras, and Nicaragua. They undertook to establish a common market within five years, abolishing internal tariffs on most of the products originating in their countries and adopting a single external tariff, which has already largely been negotiated. Assurance of internal free trade is expected to act as a strong stimulus to Central America's industrial growth, and to reach this objective as rapidly as possible, financial institutions have been set up specifically to support projects that tend to strengthen economic integration. Nevertheless, apart from the nonparticipation of Costa Rica[2] and the lack of definite arrangements with Panama, a country with similar economic characteristics, Central America still has many problems to solve. Most important is to achieve an equitable distribution of the new industrial plants that are to benefit from the common market. This will require a mechanism of positive government action, which, functioning within a multinational framework, will certainly have greater difficulty than a national development program. Although Central America's economic integration has proceeded very slowly, the awareness of the need for such a program is growing. Unquestionably, any

[2] Since this was written, Costa Rica has adhered to the free-trade and industrial integration treaties in Central America.

future policy of economic development will have to take into account the advisability of combining the economies of those small countries and ultimately forming a single economy.

It may also be hoped that the Latin American Free-Trade Association, incorporating Mexico and most South American countries, will be expanded to include Bolivia, which could enter with certain safeguards, and Venezuela, which cannot enter at present because of its critical economic situation and the high cost of many of its industries due to its overvalued currency. In any event, irrespective of the free-trade area, a considerable part of the petroleum imported by several South American countries still comes from Venezuela.

The entry of additional countries into the free-trade area will increase the benefits accruing to all members from integration, because it will multiply trade opportunities. Furthermore, countries that delay too long in joining will have to make greater initial concessions. When the Latin American common market, an expression actually not used before 1956, was first proposed, it was expected to embrace all of Latin America. Nevertheless, some South American countries never fully supported this concept, and Central America already had initiated studies designed to integrate its own economy. After it became apparent that nothing would be accomplished by insisting upon the ideal of a broad comprehensive common market, a series of "regional" integrations by groups of countries was proposed in several plans. Fortunately, it was realized that economic integration had no reason to be based on geographical proximity but could be related to the stages and prospects of industrial development. The validity of this new criterion was confirmed when Mexico joined the South American countries in their proposal of a free-trade area, and following the first negotiations in September, 1961, with the publication of long lists of products for which tariff barriers would be reduced in the free-trade area. But there is still the problem of widening the scope of the eventual area of the Central American group, including Panama and, if possible, the

Antilles. Different suggestions have been made of ways to associate the Central American group with the free-trade area created by the Montevideo Treaty and to permit individual members of each group to enter into special arrangements with the other group or parts of it, in order to expand intra-Latin American trade possibilities.[3] But at present, it seems somewhat premature to complicate further an already difficult undertaking: the formation of an area of effective reciprocal free trade that will liberalize trade in more than just a few products.

The machinery provided by the Montevideo Treaty is simple in concept but very complex in practice. The member countries of the free-trade area undertake to conduct annual negotiations to reduce by 8 per cent the weighted average tariff applicable to imports from countries outside the area. Although member countries bind themselves to reduce the *weighted* average by the percentage specified, they are free to negotiate greater reductions on some products than on others, and to add to the negotiations new products not already traded. In this way, no country is obliged to open completely its customs borders to products of other members; it must only grant them a preference that can and should increase annually, so that in twelve years substantially all trade will have been liberalized. It might be thought that so gradual a process of trade liberalization, which for some products will represent very slight annual changes in the customs tariff, would offer little incentive to industrial expansion. It has been remarked that the Montevideo Treaty contains numerous safeguard clauses that permit a country to impose direct restrictions on imports of products already partially liberalized, and to make special arrangements in the trade of agricultural commodities. But if a country grants a tariff reduction on a product, it is obliged to extend that concession to all other members of

[3] OAS, *The Economic Integration of Latin America*, Report of the Group of Experts, Topic II of the Agenda of the Special Meeting of the Inter-American Economic and Social Council at the Ministerial Level. Doc. OEA/Ser.H/X.1, ES-RE-Doc.3, August, 1961.

the free-trade area; and, conversely, if a country obtains a tariff reduction, the other countries will automatically enjoy the same advantage. It is sometimes hard to imagine how much a multilateral mechanism of negotiation differs from the purely bilateral procedure traditionally used by Latin American countries. The net result of all this complicated process might be, and unquestionably is intended to be, much more stimulating to intra-Latin American trade than many have believed possible. Furthermore, as in Europe, the member countries may decide to shorten the stages of trade liberalization.[4]

The Montevideo Treaty and the process of Latin American integration present many other financial and technical problems that cannot be gone into at this time.[5] It is interesting, however, to consider two very important aspects: first, whether Latin American economic integration will reduce or increase the evident inequalities in the development levels of the different countries; second, whether it will help or hinder the programming of Latin American economic development.

As regards the first question, it may be observed that striking disparities in living standards and development levels exist not only between different countries but also *within* most countries. Underdevelopment is a generalized ill that afflicts even the Latin American countries with the highest living standards. Inevitably, some regions within a country develop more rapidly and effectively than others, thanks to resources, population, the concentrated effect of external demand, or other advantages. According to François Perroux and Albert O. Hirschman, a certain measure of polarization is necessary to development. But if it goes too far

[4] The first multilateral negotiations of the LAFTA were concluded in December, 1961. The reciprocal tariff reductions agreed upon entered into force on January 1, 1962. A further round of negotiations took place late in 1962 and a third set was scheduled for October, 1963.

[5] In *Free Trade and Economic Integration in Latin America* (Berkeley, University of California Press, 1962), the author has dealt extensively with these topics, and with the background of the Montevideo Treaty and the Central American agreements. The ECLA's ample documentation on these subjects should also be consulted.

it should be blamed not so much on the existence of a free-trade area or common market as on the particular programming of national economic development. If this includes measures to raise the more backward regions both socially and economically and to incorporate them into the general development, there is no reason to suppose that they could not benefit from the added dimension furnished by Latin American integration. If there was no programming or if it was indifferent to the inequality between different regions of the country or different sectors of the economy, the impact of the free-trade area could intensify the inequality. No nation should blindly commit itself to integration with other countries unless it already understands its own economic development and its problems, which once again poses the necessity of programming development.

When a less advanced country has drawn up its development program, it will be able to appraise and take utmost advantage of the possibilities for executing its program that are offered by the common market or the free-trade area. Moreover, the Montevideo Treaty accords the weaker countries generally more favorable treatment and assistance in solving their problems. Consequently, the less advanced countries have nothing to lose and much to gain from integration; also, they probably will receive substantial foreign aid for economic development.

The second aspect that merits special examination is the relation between the integration of the Latin American economies and the over-all programming of economic development. For some time, it has been suggested that an over-all programming of the Latin American economy would be desirable. The more advanced countries, in the first place, should help the weaker or less industrialized countries. But, second, the combined development programs of several countries should signify more than the aggregation of investments and production targets. If the programs of some countries are linked to those of others, their execution automatically will fit into the concept of programmed integration for Latin America. Relating integration to a coordinated program seems easy, but it certainly will be a long, slow, and complicated process. Partial problems concerning two neighboring countries or an economic sector of common interest may be worked out, but there can be no hope of over-all economic programming for Latin America until the idea of programming has been wholly accepted in each country. Nonetheless, as the free-trade area helps advance integration, it will become increasingly clear that important branches of industry, as well as other aspects of the economy, should be coordinated. The advisability of such coordination is already recognized to some extent by the steel, chemical, and other industries.

There is no doubt that the first determined, realistic steps have been taken toward integration of the Latin American economies, and that the latter can contribute significantly to accelerated economic development, provided other conditions—economic, social, and political—are met. The next and final chapter will recapitulate these conditions, already discussed separately, and consider particularly the climate of international cooperation that would most favor them.

11. The Alliance for Progress and Latin American Development

IN THE LAST twenty years, during which Latin America has become increasingly aware of the problems of development and convinced that it must act vigorously to solve them, false hopes have been created by periods of prosperity. The Latin American economy emerged from World War II generally strengthened, and as appreciable amounts of capital goods became available, its growth was quickened. Nevertheless, some markets for primary products soon began to weaken and accumulated savings meanwhile were wasted in part on unnecessary imports. The terms of trade deteriorated and balance-of-payments difficulties and internal equilibrium problems became more acute. Many development programs and major projects were left unfinished or were delayed; some important sectors of public services and industry did not expand swiftly enough; agriculture and livestock raising, barring exceptional cases, were relatively neglected; petroleum and iron ore continued to find markets, but mining, which had been stimulated by the war, otherwise came to a standstill.

During the Inter-American Conference on Problems of War and Peace (the Chapultepec Conference), held in Mexico in 1945, the majority of the Latin American countries stated very clearly that the postwar period presented two types of interrelated problems: external instability and development. To achieve an understanding with the United States in economic matters, Latin America stressed the need for increased stability, a careful transition to new conditions of supply and demand in primary products and financial aid to development and industrialization.[1] These forms of cooperation assumed even more importance in the light of Europe's slow economic recovery and diminished trade with Latin America. The Latin American countries did not speak with a single voice; worse yet, their words fell on deaf ears. According to the United States, price instability would be solved by the free play of market forces, international financing would be provided by private capital, and industrialization should not be given any special incentives, much less tariff protection. The momentum of the wartime boom was judged sufficient to carry Latin America back to a kind of normalcy.

Three years later, the United States attitude had not changed, at the World Trade and Employment Conference, held in Havana, or at the Bogotá Inter-American Conference, when Latin America repeated its stand on the economic problems that confronted it and were beginning to take on alarming proportions. Represented by the Secretary of State whose name had been given to his country's four-year program of aid to European recovery, the United States informed Latin America that it was in no position to divert its attention from the Marshall Plan and its other commitments to the countries of Europe and Asia, and recommended that, rather than request loans, Latin America should devote itself to creating favorable conditions for foreign private investment. Furthermore, it was expected that the recently established International Bank for Reconstruction and Development, together with a small increase in the capital of the Export-Import Bank, would suffice to meet the principal requests for long-term loans.[2]

At that time, various Latin American circles began to discuss the possibility of persuading the United States to create a sort of

[1] See the author's article "Problemas económicos planteados en la Conferencia de Chapultepec," *Boletín del Banco Central de Venezuela* (Caracas), IV, No. 16 (April, 1945), 32–40.
[2] See, for example, the account given by Eduardo Villaseñor in "El Banco Interamericano," *El Trimestre Económico*, XV, No. 58 (July–September, 1948), particularly pp. 184–85.

Marshall Plan for Latin America. But no definite proposal was ever made. It must be remembered that the countries of Western Europe knew what they wanted, that many of them had drawn up fairly detailed plans for postwar recovery and development, and that with the help of the Organization for European Economic Cooperation they were able quickly to put their plans into operation. But, excluding Perón's misguided policies, Latin America lacked programs and even a well-thought-out orientation; nor did it derive much benefit from inter-American agencies.

With the economic impact of the Korean War and the rise in the price of coffee, many difficulties were forgotten and once again there was the illusion that the problems of Latin American development could be solved easily without massive international cooperation. United States insistence on the civilizing mission of foreign private investment had found supporters in two or three Latin American countries, and total figures for private capital movements did increase considerably, even though, as seen in Chapter 4, they were concentrated in petroleum and mining. The expanded operations of the World Bank and the Eximbank, and the high prices for coffee and other products enabled many countries to undertake new and ambitious projects. But these conditions did not last long, and the United States economic recession in late 1953 and early 1954 brought back into sharp relief the serious, chronic problems confronting the Latin American economy.

During this period, the inter-American conferences, then primarily dedicated to examining political problems, accomplished practically nothing. The Tenth Inter-American Conference, held in Caracas in 1954, which referred economic problems to a special meeting of ministers of economy and finance scheduled for the end of the year, only added to Latin America's mounting dissatisfaction with the economic and other policies of the United States. Nevertheless, in a time of great misunderstanding and frequent obstructions, the problems of Latin American economic development were the subject of a thorough study by the ECLA. From this emerged a body of principles for a Latin American policy of economic growth. This systematic and patient labor, free of prejudices and illusions, based on harsh reality, far from the diplomatic intrigues of Washington, sober and competent, was carried out by the Secretariat of the Economic Commission for Latin America, under the direction of Raúl Prebisch, an outstanding economist possessed of a breadth of vision rarely found in a Latin American. When the economic conference convened in Petrópolis, Brazil, the ECLA was ready with a groundwork of ideas, principles, and recommendations on which to build a new concept of United States cooperation in Latin American development.[3]

The ECLA report rested on a skilful examination of the problems of growth and stability in the Latin American economy and made clear that any solution would require several different approaches. One should be a substantial increase in long-term financing, partly through creation of an inter-American fund for the development of industry, agriculture, and mining. Foreign-capital requirements were estimated at one billion dollars a year, a sum now considered modest, of which about $700 million should come from international credit sources. At the same time, however, the Latin American countries, in order to absorb more foreign capital, were to adopt well-defined national programs of development. Such programs should include, among others, the following elements: a considerable expansion of infrastructural and other basic investments, particularly those resulting in rapid gains in productivity; suitable orientation of foreign private investment; adequate economic programming machinery; and monetary, fiscal, tariff, and other measures to mobilize domestic savings and create incentives for growth. The program of Latin American development and the policy of inter-American coopera-

[3] ECLA. *International Cooperation in a Latin American Development Policy* (United Nations, New York, 1954, Publ. 54, II. G.2). The recommendations of this report served, in fact, as draft resolutions or as the basis for discussions, although few were finally accepted.

tion should, according to these proposals, be reviewed periodically. The preparation of national plans could be aided, at the request of any country, by an advisory group made up of impartial and competent personnel.

To mitigate the effects of short-run fluctuations, the ECLA report urged adoption of international measures designed to compensate for exchange losses or price falls; it also recommended formation of internal reserves during periods of prosperity which, supplemented by external loans, would keep development projects going during periods of exchange shortage.

The development program was also conceived of as a body of measures to promote industrialization and improve agriculture through foreign-trade policy. It called for Latin America to practice a moderate degree of protectionism, and for the United States, without demanding equivalent concessions, to open its markets to Latin American products and work toward eliminating specific obstacles to its increased consumption of such commodities. The same report also suggested guidelines for liberalizing intra-Latin American trade, which foreshadowed the present free-trade area.

The scarcity of trained technical personnel and the technological inferiority of national enterprise were also dealt with, together with the advisability of programming an optimal use of international technical assistance.

Thus, in 1954, the ECLA defined the fundamental problems of economic development, both internal and as related to inter-American trade and financial cooperation. These same problems still exist, and they again arose at the Punta del Este economic conference of August, 1961. Furthermore, the ECLA described them in the light of political and social realities, recognizing the functions that governments must assume to solve them effectively within a mixed public and private economy. But the only positive result of that inter-American economic conference held in Petrópolis in November, 1954, was the adoption of a resolution— the United States and Peru abstained—to set up a committee of experts to draft a proposal for a financial development institution or an inter-American bank.[4] General recommendations were also made on programming and on development policy.[5] The rest was rejected by the United States or diluted in resolutions of little or no significance. The United States, like the World Bank, was particularly opposed to setting any quantitative goal of international financial cooperation or to formulating programs of economic development.

It became increasingly clear that the Government and influential private circles of the United States had no comprehension of the true nature of Latin America's problems. Economic and political relations between the United States and Latin America deteriorated to the point where, in 1957, the OAS economic conference in Buenos Aires was a total failure, and in 1958, the U.S. Vice President was attacked physically in two Latin American capitals during a good-will tour. These events, added to the growing economic difficulties in almost all Latin American countries, prompted President Kubitschek of Brazil to suggest to President Eisenhower in May, 1958, that there was need for a "thorough reappraisal" of inter-American relations, in consultation with the other governments.[6] Although President Eisenhower's reply displayed more concern with international political solidarity than with the economic situation,[7] it favored carrying out the consultations. The Brazilian idea, presented in both political and economic terms, acquired more substance a few

[4] See *Meeting of Ministers of Finance or Economy, as the Fourth Extraordinary Meeting of the Inter-American Economic and Social Council of the Organization of American States, held at Petrópolis from November 22 to December 2, 1954.* Resolution No. 40.

[5] *Ibid.* Resolutions 32 and 46.

[6] Letter from President Juscelino Kubitschek to President Dwight D. Eisenhower, May 28, 1958. See U.S. Department of State, *Bulletin*, XXXVIII, No. 992 (June 30, 1958), 1091.

[7] Letter from President Eisenhower to President Kubitschek, June 5, 1958 (*ibid.*, pp. 1090–91): "There is a wide range of subjects to be discussed and explored, including, for example, the problem of implementing more fully the Declaration of Solidarity of the Tenth Inter-American Conference held at Caracas in 1954."

weeks later when President Kubitschek announced that if Latin America was to "participate actively in problems that are world-wide in scope," it would have to promote economic development and launch a massive program to eliminate poverty.[8] He conceived of the program as a series of measures to intensify investment in Latin America's backward regions, increase technical assistance, stabilize the prices of primary products, and expand the inflow of financial resources from abroad. This was the beginning of Operation Pan America, which the Brazilian President did not compare with the much more comprehensive Marshall Plan, but described, instead, as a new force based on cooperation and understanding, and on the premise that Pan Americanism "had barely advanced a few inches in the field of economic accomplishments."[9]

The United States attitude toward the proposed Operation Pan America was set forth for the first time in a speech by Secretary of State Dulles in Rio de Janeiro in August, 1958, when he stated that his government was concerned with problems of economic cooperation, but warned that "the economic well-being of a nation always depends primarily on its own efforts . . . requires a stable political order . . . sound fiscal, monetary and taxation practices . . . that the people freely accept self-discipline, hard work and frugality . . . ," and he declared that the United States "will expand its efforts to help all the American Republics help themselves to achieve economic strength under freedom."[10] A joint communiqué issued at Brasília by the governments of Brazil and the United States reaffirmed the political principles of inter-

[8] Speech by President Kubitschek to the nation and to the diplomatic representatives of the American states, June 20, 1958. See *Operación Panamericana. Compilación de Documentos* (Rio de Janeiro, Presidencia de la República, Servicio de Documentación, 1958), I, 31–37. (Spanish text.)

[9] From an interview given by President Kubitschek to *The New York Times,* June 6, 1958.

[10] Speech by Secretary of State John Foster Dulles to the American Chamber of Commerce in Rio de Janeiro, August 6, 1958. U.S. Department of State, *Bulletin,* XXXIX, No. 1000 (August 25, 1958), 307.

American solidarity and "their convictions that the strengthening of the American community requires, among other measures, dynamic efforts to overcome the problems of underdevelopment."[11]

The idea of Operation Pan America was immediately accepted and supported by a number of countries, among them Argentina, Colombia, and Paraguay. The Brazilian Government outlined for all a plan to convene a Special Committee of the Organization of American States—later referred to as the Committee of Twenty-one—to examine the general objectives of a broad program of economic and financial cooperation incorporating new bases for international credit; the creation of an inter-American financial institution; measures to encourage private investment, combat inflation, and stabilize markets; the use of technical assistance; and the study of means to cope with the consequences of the European Common Market and to develop "regional markets" on the American continent.[12]

In September, 1958, during an informal meeting of the foreign ministers of the Latin American republics held in Washington, D.C., Brazil made a clear and accurate presentation of the problems of Latin American development and of the way in which they might be solved,[13] but it met with various political objections. Brazil argued that Latin America needed substantial foreign aid to raise its income within a twenty-year period from $270 to $400 per capita at 1950 prices (a compound growth rate of 4.4 per cent involving a gross investment ratio of more than 20 per cent of the gross national product). Once the $400 level was reached, it was hoped that national resources alone could sustain a steady rise in income. In their declaration, the Latin

---

[11] Declaration of Brasília, August 6, 1958 (*ibid.*, p. 301).

[12] *Pro memoria* submitted to the diplomatic missions of the American republics, Rio de Janeiro, August 9, 1958. See *Operación Panamericana. Compilación de Documentos*, II, 97–106.

[13] *Aide-mémoire* presented by the Brazilian Government to the American delegations, Washington, D.C., September 22, 1958 (*ibid.*, III, 85–101).

American Foreign Ministers in Washington supported Operation Pan America only in a general way, by endorsing an examination of its proposals by the Committee of Twenty-one. Nevertheless, they did recommend creation of an "Inter-American economic development institution" (the Inter-American Development Bank).[14]

The Committee of Twenty-one met in Washington in November, 1958, and received from the Brazilian delegation a searching analysis of the problems of the Latin American economy, together with formulas for an over-all program. This relied on ample external financial aid, of which a large part would have to be public in origin, since private sources could not be expected to contribute an adequate amount.[15] The delegation emphasized that quantitative targets should be fixed, and it indicated that Brazil alone would need $3 billion over the next twenty years (and that all of Latin America might need as much as $10 billion).[16]

At the same time, Brazil continued to stress the political character of Operation Pan America. President Kubitschek sent a message to the Committee of Twenty-one in which he stated that, "more than a study of economic solutions, Operation Pan America pursues a loftier objective—to affirm some principles and renew attitudes in the face of the crisis that threatens our way of life and the democratic system."[17] In a speech given in Asunción in August of that year, the Brazilian foreign minister had

[14] Communiqué of the Meeting of the Foreign Ministers of the American Republics, Washington, D.C., September 24, 1958 (*The New York Times,* September 25, 1958).

[15] Speech by Augusto Federico Schmidt, Brazil's representative on the Committee of Twenty-one, November 25, 1958 (*Operación Panamericana. Compilación de Documentos,* IV, 51–79). See also his speech on December 4, 1958 (*ibid.,* pp. 97–107).

[16] This last figure was mentioned by President Kubitschek in an address delivered before the War College of Rio de Janeiro, November 26, 1958 (*ibid.,* IV, 91).

[17] Message from President Kubitschek to the Committee of Twenty-one, Rio de Janeiro, November 17, 1958 (*ibid.,* IV, 17–19).

said that "the objective . . . is, above all, one of a politico-strategic nature."[18]

In the Committee of Twenty-one, the United States showed considerable reserve toward the idea of a Latin American plan for development. A U.S. representative pointed out that an overall plan would offer "too many variables in the equation" and that it was preferable to begin with specific problems and, in any case, with national plans;[19] another U.S. delegate stated, after listing the activities of various United States and international financial agencies, that "public lending . . . can never substitute for private initiative and private capital. . . . We need to clear away the obstacles to the entry of private capital into the countries desiring investment, and provide, in greater degree, positive incentives to increased investment. . . . What is required is the maintenance of a hospitable atmosphere in which private enterprise can operate with confidence."[20] Furthermore, the United States Government offered to support the stabilization of the prices of primary products only to the extent of being "ready to join in the study of individual commodity problems which are creating difficulties to see whether cooperative solutions can be found."[21]

Whether because of the political aspects of Operation Pan America or because of United States' skepticism, the Brazilians did not obtain the support they sought for their proposals. Aside from the resolution to establish a group of experts to draw up the statutes of the future Inter-American Bank, the Committee of Twenty-one produced nothing concrete. The report of the

[18] Speech by the Brazilian Foreign Minister, Francisco Negrão de Lima, Asunción, Paraguay, August 16, 1958 (*ibid.*, II, 86). See also the *pro-memoria* cited in footnote 12: "Operation Pan America should be regarded as a corollary to the general strategy of the West . . ." (*ibid.*, p. 99).

[19] Speech by Thomas Mann, alternate representative of the United States, November 2, 1958 (*ibid.*, V, 83–87).

[20] Speech by Douglas C. Dillon, United States representative, November 18, 1958. U.S. Department of State, *Bulletin*, XXXIX, No. 1015 (December 8, 1958), 919.

[21] *Ibid.*, p. 921.

Brazilian delegation to its government revealed its disappointment in, and even criticism of, the position taken by the other Latin American governments.[22] Subsequently, a working group was set up in the OAS to present a series of more specific draft resolutions to a second meeting of the Committee of Twenty-one in Buenos Aires. The Brazilian Government, recognizing that the Committee had at least created a climate and an orientation for Operation Pan America, further defined some of its ideas on development programming and tried to make clear in its political declarations that Latin America's integration in Western efforts to guarantee peace was not to be interpreted as an identification with Anglo-American foreign policy or with NATO.[23]

The working group, having abandoned the concept of a global program for Latin America or of quantitative goals, recommended that studies be carried out by countries;[24] and in the second meeting of the Committee of Twenty-one, a joint declaration acknowledged that economic problems were as important and as urgent as political problems and those relating to mutual security. Although the idea of a new policy of inter-American cooperation in economic matters was reaffirmed, its sole expression remained the Inter-American Bank project. It was in this conference that the Cuban delegation estimated at $30 billion the Latin American foreign capital requirements for a ten-year development program, and announced that a solution to the problem of land tenure, education, and income distribution was indispensable to development. The Committee of Twenty-one established a subcommittee that was to submit its studies on Operation Pan America to the Eleventh Inter-American Conference, scheduled to take place in Quito, Ecuador, in 1959.

22 First Report of the Brazilian delegation on the Committee of Twenty-one, Rio de Janeiro, January 20, 1959. *Operación Panamericana. Compilación de Documentos*, V, 143–706.

23 *Ibid.*, p. 151.

24 Summary of the Second Report of the Brazilian delegation on the Committee of Twenty-one, Rio de Janeiro, April 8, 1959 (*ibid.*, VII, 49-71, especially pp. 53–54).

This conference was postponed and finally canceled. In the months that followed, Operation Pan America, no longer offering an over-all program and goals, apparently lost its initial momentum.

The next stage, after Cuba veered toward the Soviet bloc, was characterized by growing U.S. concern over the social aspects of development, which, it is interesting to note, had not figured in either the ECLA's 1954 recommendations or in Operation Pan America. President Eisenhower's tour through several Latin American countries in March, 1960, evidenced a new political point of view.[25] Meanwhile, the Inter-American Bank had commenced operations and the United States Government began to change its attitude about the most suitable forms of financing Latin American development.

At its third meeting, which resulted in the Act of Bogotá in September, 1960, the OAS Committee of Twenty-one decided "to give further practical expression to the spirit of Operation Pan America by immediately enlarging the opportunities of the people of Latin America for social progress," and it generally recognized the interdependence of social and economic progress.[26] In this respect, the Act of Bogotá indicated that economic development could not be carried out unless inter-American programs were undertaken to improve rural living and land use and tenure, housing, education, health, and tax systems. Together with the idea of social reform, much emphasis was placed on an oft-repeated United States conviction, first expressed two years earlier in its comments on Operation Pan America,[27] that the success of external aid was contingent on the existence of national programs based on the principle of self-help and the maximum use of domestic resources. These ideas resulted in an agreement by the United States Government to allocate an additional half

25 José Garrido Torres, "El imperativo urgente de la cooperación económica interamericana," *Foro Internacional*, I, No. 4 (April–June, 1960), particularly pp. 583–5.
26 Preamble to the Act of Bogotá, September 12, 1960.
27 See footnote 10.

billion dollars to create a Special Fund for Social Development, to be administered by the Inter-American Bank and used to finance, on flexible and adequate terms, projects of social significance that Latin American countries might wish to initiate as part of general programs of reforming their institutions and utilizing their resources.[28] As is well known, the Fund is already operating through a trust account set up in the Inter-American Bank by the United States Government.

The Act of Bogotá also adopted a new approach to financing development that represented a sharp departure from traditional United States policy. It made clear that within the framework of Operation Pan America and as an expression of the latter, "the economic development of Latin America requires prompt action of exceptional breadth in the field of international cooperation and domestic effort," and for this purpose, it recommended a program of "additional public and private financial assistance on the part of capital-exporting countries of America, Western Europe, and international lending agencies," with special attention to the need for loans on more flexible terms and conditions, including foreign financing for the coverage of local expenditures and longer repayment schedules.[29] Consequently, by the end of 1960, avenues of easier access to the external financing of Latin American development began to open up. In addition to the Inter-American Fund for Social Development, the United States was prepared to urge a greater flow of loans on suitable terms and conditions from both its own credit and financial agencies and from international and European institutions. Meanwhile, the World Bank and the Eximbank increased the total amount of their loanable funds. Significantly, in the Act of Bogotá, for the first time no mention was made of foreign private capital as the preferred instrument for financing Latin American development nor was it suggested that the primary purpose of Latin American

28 Act of Bogotá, Part II.
29 *Ibid.*, Part III.

discussions should be the creation of a favorable climate for such investment.

The Act of Bogotá was the basis for the still more encouraging policy announced during the 1960 election campaign as the "Alliance for Progress" and subsequently pursued by President Kennedy's Administration. The United States envisaged the Alliance not as a plan simply to alleviate social pressures and accentuate economic advances, but as a pacific and positive revolution aimed at transforming the social and economic structure of Latin America; and as a plan in which Europe, Canada, and Japan, as well as the United States, would cooperate with large-scale technical and financial resources, provided that the Latin American countries undertook to intensify, as needed, broadly conceived and really progressive programs. Although the Alliance for Progress adopted some of the development and financial goals outlined by Operation Pan America, it went far beyond the latter in general concepts, and laid much less stress on immediate political aspects; and in its social and economic concepts it went further than even the provisions of the Act of Bogotá. President Kennedy, speaking at the White House in March, 1961, hailed the Alliance for Progress as a "vast cooperative effort, unparalleled in magnitude and nobility of purpose, to satisfy the basic needs of the American people," and he proposed among other things, the launching of a ten-year plan that would constitute "the years of maximum progress, maximum effort—the years when the greatest obstacles must be overcome, the years when the need for assistance will be greatest."[30]

Since Latin America had been discussing for many years its problems and the forms of cooperation needed to solve them, these ideas had had time to mature and take definite shape. Furthermore, United States acceptance of Latin American view-

[30] Address by President John F. Kennedy to the Latin American diplomatic corps, March 13, 1961. U.S. Department of State, *Bulletin*, XLIV, No. 1136 (April 3, 1961), 472.

points meant that the Special Meeting of the Inter-American Economic and Social Council at the Ministerial Level, convened in August, 1961, faced an easier task than had many previous conferences. The Declaration and the Charter of Punta del Este are documents that in fact embody all the elements until then considered essential to a Latin American development program.

The Declaration reinforces the earlier Act of Bogotá by including in its commitments references to remuneration for work performed and to labor-management relations, and it clearly specifies such instruments of progress as integral land reform, fiscal reform, Latin American economic integration, and other policies aimed at economic and social improvement.[31] It also states that the United States "pledges its efforts to supply financial and technical cooperation in order to achieve the aims of the Alliance for Progress" and that "to this end, the United States will provide a major part of the minimum of $20 billion, principally in public funds, which Latin America will require over the next ten years from all external sources in order to supplement its own efforts." As an immediate contribution, the United States indicated that it would provide more than $1 billion during the twelve months beginning on March 13, 1961. It also announced its intention of furnishing "development loans on a long-term basis, where appropriate running up to fifty years and in general at very low or zero rates of interest." For their part, the countries of Latin America agreed to devote a steadily increasing share of their own resources to economic and social development, "to make the reforms necessary to assure that all share fully in the fruits of the Alliance for Progress," and to formulate in each country national development programs for the purposes of the new policy of cooperation.[32]

31 Declaration to the Peoples of America. See OAS, *Alliance for Progress. Official Documents Emanating from the Special Meeting of the Inter-American Economic and Special Council at the Ministerial Level,* Punta del Este, August 5–17, 1961. (OAS/Ser. H/X.1, Doc. ES-RE-Doc. 145, August 16, 1961.)
32 *Ibid.*

The Charter of Punta del Este[33] establishes a quantitative goal which, although not as ambitious as that of Operation Pan America, is fairly high: an annual rate of economic growth of not less than 2.5 per cent per capita during the ten years ending in 1971 (requiring a gross investment ratio of about 17 per cent). Each country is to determine its own growth target, recognizing the need to work toward a better distribution of income and to effect the indispensable changes in structure and production, especially through industrialization. Among the qualitative goals named in the Charter are those relating to education, health, agrarian reform, housing, progressive taxation, stability of the prices of primary products, and Latin American integration.

To achieve the objective of an annual 2.5 per cent per capita growth rate—almost as high as the 1945–55 average, which subsequently declined to a little more than 1.5 per cent per year—the Charter of Punta del Este commits each country to formulate within eighteen months long-term development programs that would not be mere lists of projects, but would embody a group of targets and appropriate instruments aimed at raising productivity, fully exploiting resources and improving living conditions. Thus, development programming is made a condition of external financial support, as it is believed that external financing cannot be effectively utilized unless internal resources are rationally employed. While long-term programs are in preparation, the Charter of Punta del Este establishes immediate action objectives to accelerate the financing of projects designed to meet social needs, mobilize idle resources, and facilitate execution of long-term programs.

The Punta del Este Conference also gave unqualified support to both the Montevideo Treaty and the Central American agreements as instruments of economic integration, with the recommendation that their programs be intensified and interrelated and with suggestions concerning special financial assistance.

[33] The Charter of Punta del Este, Establishing an Alliance for Progress Within the Framework of Operation Pan America. *Ibid.*

In the matter of education and health, resolutions were adopted recommending ten-year plans for attaining such specific objectives as literacy, universal primary education, technical and secondary education, control of disease, sanitation, and water supply. Other problems, including transport, were also dealt with.

The only topic for which the Punta del Este Conference made no well-defined provisions was the stabilization of the prices of primary products. This matter, which by its very nature presents many complicated aspects that are outside the inter-American domain, had been studied by an OAS committee of experts. The latter submitted a report urging examination of a recent proposal by a United Nations group on compensation for loss of exchange earnings due to a fall in prices.[34] Apart from making the usual recommendations on eliminating obstacles to the consumption of basic commodities in the more developed countries, the Punta del Este Conference supported only in a general way efforts to bring about international agreements on primary products; and it again set up a group of experts to consider the various stabilization proposals and to prepare a draft plan on the creation of a mechanism for compensatory financing.[35] The coffee question, on which an international agreement was already being sought through other channels, prompted a special resolution that expressed the hope that such an agreement would include provisions for export quotas and even for limitations on the planting and production of coffee.[36]

The fundamental significance of the Charter of Punta del Este is that for the first time the United States has accepted the idea that Latin America's economic and social development is an over-all problem requiring integral solutions. The Charter recog-

[34] OAS, *Latin American Export Commodities—Market Problems.* Report of the Group of Experts, Topic IV of the Agenda, Special Meeting of the Inter-American Economic and Social Council at the Ministerial Level. Doc. ES-RE-5. Washington, D.C., July, 1961. See also Chapter 5, *supra.*

[35] Charter of Punta del Este, Title IV, Chap. II.

[36] Charter of Punta del Este, Appendix, Resolution C.1.

nizes the need for a massive injection of external financial resources, largely in the form of loans, and it establishes minimum
goals of per capita income growth—2.5 per cent per annum—
and of external financing—$20 billion in ten years. According to
the United States Secretary of the Treasury,[37] in an approximate
breakdown of the $2 billion of foreign aid to be assigned annually
to Latin American economic development, some $400 million
would be furnished by the United States Export-Import Bank,
$250 million by the social-development program formulated in
the Act of Bogotá, about $150 million by the Food for Peace
Program, $75 million by the Development Loan Fund of the
United States Government, $75 million by technical-assistance
agencies, and $750 million would take the form of loans from
international organizations, including the Inter-American Bank,
and public loans and private investment by Western Europe and
Japan. It is estimated that United States private capital would
represent only the remaining $300 million.

Not only does the United States no longer urge that private
foreign capital be the preferred instrument of financing, but it
accepts and even advises that economic development be planned,
thus acknowledging the value of the ECLA's long-standing recommendations on programming. The Charter of Punta del Este
even makes provisions for close cooperation by the OAS, ECLA,
and the Inter-American Bank in giving technical advice to those
countries that request it in preparing their long-term programs.

Another significant aspect of the Charter of Punta del Este is
that financial cooperation is conditioned by whether social reforms are carried out concurrently with economic development
projects. The social backwardness of broad areas of Latin
America and the ineffectiveness of many of the agrarian, educational, and other programs have been recognized as serious obstacles to growth. The United States is justified in observing that
in the past the financial aid given to many countries has not

[37] Address delivered by the United States Secretary of the Treasury Douglas
C. Dillon before the World Affairs Council, Los Angeles, September 11, 1961.

resulted in solid economic and social advances; in the beneficiary countries, a wealthy minority have sent abroad for safekeeping large sums of domestic capital. The Charter of Punta del Este represents a new approach to the intensification of basic social programs.

Another characteristic of the Punta del Este plan is worth pointing out. In no way does it restrict a Latin American country's freedom to associate, through trade or investment, with any other country. Unlike previous formulas that envisaged an exclusive association between Latin America and the United States, the Charter provisions embrace participation in Latin American development by Europe, Canada, Japan, or any other country. Furthermore, an important part of the resources will come from international agencies. And no prohibition or limitation is imposed on economic relations with the Soviet bloc, which undoubtedly will expand its trade and might provide an outlet for surpluses in certain basic products in exchange for equipment. However, the Charter of Punta del Este apparently does not allow a country to have free access to the resources of the Alliance for Progress plan if it adopts a political system that is not based on democratic representation or if it links itself exclusively to the Soviet bloc. This is currently the situation of Cuba, which has made its economic and social development dependent on the program of trade, loans, and other aid offered by the Soviet bloc. Cuba, like other Latin American countries, needs to sell what it produces, and, for its national program of economic development, it requires the cooperation of countries that want to buy its exports and that, having a relatively high level of industrialization, can grant it credit for machinery and industrial equipment. In this sense, Cuba has also obtained aid for development, but by traveling along a very different political road.

What can be expected from the Alliance for Progress? The figures cited are less important than the way in which external support for and cooperation with Latin America are envisaged. The Alliance for Progress resembles the Marshall Plan in guaranteeing sufficient foreign funds to assure the success of domestic effort, so long as the region lives up to its responsibilities. No program of international cooperation will succeed in Latin America if skepticism prevails; if governments insist on proclaiming, as has already occurred, that nothing remains to be done to comply with the objectives of the Alliance; if long-term economic programs are merely lists of projects; and if institutional, political and social deficiencies are not corrected. If this happens, the failure will be Latin America's. But if, after Latin America embarks on this new stage of development, external cooperation turns out to be inadequate because of shifts or halts in United States policy, the failure will be due to factors beyond its control. No objectives can be attained unless the commitment is firm and lasting on both sides. The situation must be examined and revised periodically, as provided for, to avoid discouragement and errors in orientation.

A realistic examination of the problems and characteristics of economic development in Latin America, within a contemporary world setting, will certainly reveal that, notwithstanding the advances made in many countries, there are still formidable economic, social, and political obstacles standing in the way of development. But there will also be found ample evidence that the difficulties can be overcome, provided that the problems are recognized and defined, and that they are dealt with energetically and with the conviction that a solidly based and cumulative social process will be built up. At the present stage of Latin American development, it is imperative that social and institutional reforms be brought up to date, and that economic problems be met with technically conceived solutions that will be skillfully executed and, above all, integrated into over-all plans. Paradoxically, although Latin America hesitates to enter into a genuine program of development, the longer such a program is postponed, the more drastic, and therefore less acceptable to democratic principles, programming will have to be when it is finally initiated.

Possibly Latin America never before has enjoyed a combination of external circumstances so favorable to converting its utopias into reality—a rather imperfect reality, but many times better than the present. It is useless to pretend that ideal solutions are possible. Development, with or without support from abroad, is an arduous task and, unfortunately, slow to yield results. Raúl Prebisch has written that "development has to be brought about by our own efforts and our own determination to introduce fundamental changes in the economic and social structure of our countries. . . . A policy of international cooperation cannot be inspired by the desire to favor privileged groups within our countries or to preserve the present order of things; its objective should be to help Latin American countries to change the existing order so that economic development will be speeded up and its fruits enjoyed by the broad masses of the population."[38] The Alliance for Progress is conceived of in these terms, and actually it is the only road open to Latin America that guarantees us democracy, liberty, and personal dignity.

[38] Raúl Prebisch, "Joint Responsibilities for Latin American Progress," *Foreign Affairs*, XXXIX, No. 4 (July, 1961), 622.

Statistical Appendix

TABLE 1

POPULATION OF LATIN AMERICA, 1950-80[a]

Country	Thousands of Inhabitants				Percentage of Total			Annual Rate of Growth		Number of Years to Double Population (Base: 1960)
	1950	1960	1962	1980	1960	1962	1980	1951-1960	1961-1980	
Latin America	155,423	199,492[b]	209,812	333,296	100.0	100.0	100.0	2.5	2.6	27
Argentina	17,189	20,998	21,773	29,388	10.5	10.4	8.8	2.0	1.7	41
Bolivia	3,019	3,709	3,877	6,000	1.9	1.8	1.8	2.1	2.4	28
Brazil	51,976	65,862	69,196	109,095	33.0	33.0	32.7	2.4	2.6	27
Chile	6,073	7,634	8,001	12,000	3.8	3.8	3.6	2.3	2.3	30
Colombia	11,334	14,771	15,622	26,300	7.4	7.4	7.9	2.7	2.9	24
Costa Rica	801	1,144	1,219	2,158	0.6	0.6	0.6	3.6	3.2	21
Cuba	5,508	6,819	7,107	10,175	3.4	3.4	3.1	2.2	2.0	34
Dominican Republic	2,131	2,845	3,024	5,474	1.4	1.4	1.6	2.9	3.3	21
Ecuador	3,197	4,287	4,530	7,393	2.1	2.2	2.2	3.0	2.8	25
El Salvador	1,868	2,396	2,524	4,138	1.2	1.2	1.2	2.5	2.8	25
Guatemala	2,805	3,755	3,977	6,937	1.9	1.9	2.1	3.0	3.1	22
Haiti	3,112	3,726	3,880	5,917	1.9	1.8	1.8	1.8	2.4	30
Honduras	1,428	1,932[c]	2,031	3,246	1.0	1.0	1.0	3.1	2.6	26
Mexico	25,826	34,923[c]	37,050	63,071[d]	17.5	17.7	19.0	3.1	3.0	23
Nicaragua	1,060	1,465	1,554	2,680	0.7	0.7	0.8	3.3	3.1	23
Panama	797	1,052	1,111	1,819	0.5	0.5	0.5	2.8	2.8	25
Paraguay	1,397	1,624[e]	1,682	2,500	0.8	0.8	0.8	1.5	2.2	32
Peru	8,521	10,857[e]	11,459	19,343	5.4	5.5	5.8	2.4	2.9	24
Uruguay	2,407	2,760	2,816	3,263	1.4	1.3	1.0	1.4	0.8	83
Venezuela	4,974	6,933	7,379	12,399	3.5	3.5	3.7	3.4	2.9	23
United States	152,264	179,647[f]	185,806	251,685[g]				1.7	1.7	41
Canada	13,712	17,814[f]	18,678	28,627[h]				2.7	2.4	29

Source: ECLA, *Economic Bulletin for Latin America*, V (November, 1960) Statistical Supplement, Table 2.

[a] 1950, official data; 1960, 1962, and 1980 estimates by ECLA, based on unofficial projections by United Nations and others.
[b] Adjusted to final census figure of Mexico.
[c] Final census results, 1960.
[d] Projection at 3 per cent growth rate.
[e] Official estimate.
[f] OAS, *América en cifras*, 1960. 1. *Estadísticas demográficas*, table 11-10.
[g] Projection at 1.7 per cent growth rate.
[h] Projection at 2.4 per cent growth rate.

158

TABLE 2

CHARACTERISTICS OF LATIN AMERICA POPULATION

Country	Crude Birth Rate[a]	Crude Death Rate[a]	Percentage of Population (1960)	
	(Per 1,000 Inhabitants)		Under 15 Years of Age	Rural
Argentina	24-25	8-9	30.4	32
Bolivia	41-45	18-25	41.9	63
Brazil	42-45	16-19	42.3	63
Chile	35-37	13-14	38.8	34
Colombia	44-45	15-17	44.3	52
Costa Rica	44-48	10-15	44.1	64
Cuba	30-32	10-11	36.0	45
Dominican Republic	45-50	15-20	43.9	72
Ecuador	44-48	15-17	44.0	66
El Salvador	44-48	14-18	43.1	65
Guatemala	46-52	18-25	44.7	70
Haiti	45-55	25-35	41.6	83
Honduras	44-48	15-20	42.0	75
Mexico	45-47	14-17	43.7	49[b]
Nicaragua	45-50	14-18	44.6	63
Panama	38-42	9-12	41.5	53
Paraguay	45-50	12-18	42.4	65
Peru	42-48	15-22	44.1	59
Uruguay	18-20	7-8	26.2	19
Venezuela	44-47	12-15	42.5	39
United States	24-25	9-10	32.0	36[c]
Canada	27-27	8-9	33.5	33[d]

Source: ECLA, *Economic Bulletin for Latin America*, V, Statistical Supplement, Tables 3, 5, and 6. Data for the United States and Canada from United Nations, *Demographic Yearbook, 1960*.

[a] Annual averages, 1953-57.
[b] Official estimate.
[c] 1950.
[d] 1956.

TABLE 3
GAINFULLY EMPLOYED POPULATION IN LATIN AMERICA AND OTHER AREAS

Country	Year	Popu-lation	Gainfully Employed Total (Thousands)	Male (Thousands)	Female	Percent-age of Gainfully Employed in Total
Argentina	1947	15,894	6,446	5,163	1,283	40.6
Bolivia	1950	3,019	1,222	663	559	40.4
Brazil	1950	51,976	17,336	14,631	2,705	33.3
Chile	1952	5,933	2,188	1,642	546	36.8
Colombia	1951	11,334	3,755	3,054	701	33.1
Costa Rica	1950	801	230	42	272	28.7
Cuba	1953	5,829	1,972	1,716	256	33.8
Dominican Republic	1959	2,894	1,118	941	177	38.6
Ecuador	1959	4,169	1,601	1,178	423	38.4
El Salvador	1950	1,868	654	545	109	35.0
Guatemala	1958	3,546	1,233	1,076	157	34.7
Haiti	1950	3,112	1,747	891	856	56.1
Honduras	1950	1,428	647	362	285	45.3
Mexico	1958	32,348	10,467	8,972	1,487	32.4
Nicaragua	1950	1,060	330	284	46	31.1
Panama	1950	797	264	212	52	33.1
Paraguay	1950	1,397	437	337	100	31.2
Peru	1959	9,363	3,894	2,569	1,324	41.6
Uruguay	1955	2,800	1,020	...	...	36.4
Venezuela	1950	4,974	1,706	1,403	303	34.2
United States	1958	174,064	71,284	48,802	22,482	41.0
Canada	1958	17,015	6,120	4,640	1,480	36.0
Japan	1958	92,010	44,110	26,110	18,000	47.9
Belgium	1958	9,079	3,581	2,692	889	39.4
France	1958	44,328	19,711	13,118	6,593	44.5
Germany (Federal Republic)	1957	50,669	24,277	15,420	8,857	47.9
Italy	1958	50,225	21,361	15,532	5,829	42.5
Netherlands	1956	10,884	3,993	3,139	854	36.7
Norway	1950	3,279	1,388	1,060	328	42.3
Spain	1958	29,662	11,443	9,631	1,812	38.6
Sweden	1950	7,042	3,105	2,286	819	44.1
Switzerland	1950	4,715	2,156	1,515	640	45.7
United Kingdom	1951	50,225	23,213	16,070	7,144	46.2
Yugoslavia	1953	16,937	7,849	5,169	2,680	46.3

Source: ECLA, *Economic Bulletin for Latin America*, V, Statistical Supplement, Tables 2 and 7; International Labour Organization, *Labour Statistics Yearbook 1959*, Table 1.

TABLE 4

PERCENTAGE DISTRIBUTION OF LABOR FORCE, BY PRINCIPAL ACTIVITIES, IN LATIN AMERICA, 1950

Country	Primary Production Agriculture	Mining	Industries Manufacturing	Construction	Services	Unspecified Activities
Latin America	53.1	1.1	14.5	3.7	25.3	2.4
Argentina	24.7	0.5	22.9	6.1	43.7	2.3
Bolivia	63.3	4.2	10.7	2.5	18.4	0.9
Brazil	61.1	0.7	12.8	3.9	21.2	0.3
Chile	29.8	4.8	18.5	5.5	37.6	3.8
Colombia	56.4	1.5	14.4	3.1	21.1	3.5
Costa Rica	56.4	0.3	10.6	4.1	25.7	2.9
Cuba	43.8	0.4	15.6	2.7	36.6	0.9
Dominican Republic	69.7	0.0	8.1	2.7	17.5	2.0
Ecuador	50.9	0.4	23.1	2.2	19.1	4.3
El Salvador	64.2	0.2	11.1	2.8	18.5	3.2
Guatemala	74.8	0.1	8.3	2.0	11.6	3.2
Haiti	74.4	0.0	6.6	0.8	11.5	3.7
Honduras	75.7	0.7	7.4	1.9	11.0	3.3
Mexico	57.8	1.2	12.0	2.8	21.8	4.4
Nicaragua	69.7	0.9	10.7	2.5	16.2	—
Panama	54.9	0.1	7.1	2.6	25.7	9.6
Paraguay	58.3	0.8	14.8	2.7	20.8	2.6
Peru	59.8	1.4	15.5	2.9	19.6	1.8
Uruguay	21.7	0.1	23.8	4.3	46.4	3.7
Venezuela	41.2	2.6	10.1	5.4	32.3	8.4

Source: ECLA, "Evolution of the Employment Structure in Latin America, 1945-1955," *Economic Bulletin for Latin America*, II, No. 1 (February, 1957), Table 9.

TABLE 5

ESTIMATES OF PER CAPITA GROSS DOMESTIC PRODUCT,
LATIN AMERICA AND OTHER AREAS

Country	Year	Gross Domestic Product (Thousands) of 1960 Dollars)	Population (Thousands)	Per Capita Gross Domestic Product (In 1960 Dollars)	(Index: Latin America = 100)
Latin America	1960	73,017	199,492	366	100
	1961	75,914	204,690	371	
Argentina	1960	13,085	20,998	623	170
Bolivia	1955	305	3,334	91	25
Brazil	1960	21,644	65,862	329	90
Chile	1960	2,758	7,634	361	98
Colombia	1960	5,163	14,771	350	95
Costa Rica	1959	446	1,105	403	110
Cuba	1958	2,609	6,541	399	109
Dominican Republic	1959	660	2,760	239	65
Ecuador	1959	852	4,169	204	56
El Salvador	1959	568	2,235	254	69
Guatemala	1959	659	3,652	180	49
Haiti	1955	353	3,388	104	28
Honduras	1959	371	1,888	196	53
Mexico	1960	11,729	34,923	336	92
Nicaragua		. . .	. . .	. . .	. . .
Panama	1958	382	995	384	105
Paraguay	1958	210	1,570	134	37
Peru	1960	1,588	10,857	146	40
Uruguay	1955	938	2,615	359	98
Venezuela	1960	8,090	6,933	1,166	318
United States	1960	502,400	179,647	2,976	810
Puerto Rico	1959	1,553	2,347	661	180
Canada	1960	35,500	17,814	1,993	543
France	1959	52,730	45,097	1,169	319
Germany (Federal Republic)	1960	68,825	53,373	1,290	351
Greece	1959	2,950	8,258	357	97
Italy	1959	28,449	49,052	580	158
Portugal	1959	2,215	9,053	245	67
Spain	1957	10,450	29,431	353	96
Sweden	1959	11,271	7,454	1,512	412
United Kingdom	1959	70,148	52,157	1,345	366

(continued)

Table 5 (continued)

Country	Year	Gross Domestic Product (Thousands of 1960 Dollars)	Population (Thousands)	Per Capita Gross Domestic Product	
				(In 1960 Dollars)	(Index: Latin America = 100)
India	1959	27,031	402,750	67	18
Indonesia	1959	5,836	90,300	65	18
Japan	1959	34,912	92,740	376	102
Philippines	1960	5,930	27,456	216	59
Ghana	1959	1,433	6,489	221	60
Nigeria	1956	24,633	31,834	73	20
Sudan	1955	926	10,057	92	25

Source: Gross domestic product: United Nations, *Yearbook of National Accounts Statistics, 1960*; except for Honduras, Paraguay, United States, Canada, Germany, United Kingdom, Philippines, Ghana, and Nigeria, from IMF, *International Financial Statistics*, October, 1961; Argentina, Brazil, Colombia, Chile, El Salvador, Peru, and Venezuela, from ECLA, *Economic Survey of Latin America 1960*; and Mexico, author's estimate. Population: ECLA, *Economic Bulletin for Latin America*, V (November, 1960), Statistical Supplement, Table 2; and United Nations, *Demographic Yearbook 1960*.

Methodological note: Gross domestic product converted to current dollars at prevailing rates of exchange; when given for years prior to 1960, converted to 1960 dollars by ratio of wholesale price index of United States. In the case of Honduras, Paraguay, Dominican Republic, United States, Canada, and Philippines, gross domestic product estimated from gross national product. For India, figure represents national income only; for Indonesia, gross domestic product at factor cost. Data for Argentina, Brazil, Colombia, Costa Rica, Chile, El Salvador, Peru, and Venezuela derived from figures estimated at 1950 prices.

TABLE 6

LATIN AMERICA: GROSS DOMESTIC PRODUCT, BY PRINCIPAL COUNTRIES, 1950, 1955, AND 1960

Country	Millions of Dollars (At 1950 Prices)			Percentage of Total			Annual Rate of Growth		
	1950	1955	1960[a]	1950	1955	1960	1951-55	1956-60	1951-60
Latin America	39,700	49,800	63,000	100.0	100.0	100.0	4.6	4.8	4.7
Argentina	9,889	10,936	11,290	24.9	22.0	17.9	2.0	0.6	1.3
Brazil	10,232	13,200	18,675	25.8	26.5	29.6	5.2	7.2	6.2
Chile	1,831	2,137	2,383	4.6	4.3	3.8	3.1	2.2	2.7
Colombia	2,910	3,768	4,455	7.3	7.5	7.1	5.3	3.4	4.4
Mexico[b]	5,194	7,268	9,701	13.1	14.6	15.4	7.0	6.0	6.5
Peru	1,145	1,521	1,370	2.9	3.1	2.2	5.7	-2.1	1.8
Venezuela	3,379	5,131	6,982	8.5	10.3	11.1	8.7	6.3	7.5
Sum of 7 Countries	34,580	43,961	54,856	87.1	88.3	87.1	4.9	4.5	4.7
Others	5,120	5,839	8,144	12.9	11.7	12.9	2.7	6.9	4.7

Source: Derived from ECLA, *Economic Bulletin for Latin America*, V, Statistical Supplement, Table 12; and *Economic Survey of Latin America 1960*, Part I, Table II-3.
[a]Preliminary estimates.
[b]Author's estimate.

TABLE 7

LATIN AMERICA: DISTRIBUTION OF GROSS PRODUCT AND GAINFULLY EMPLOYED POPULATION, BY ACTIVITIES, 1960

Activity	A Percentage of Gross Domestic Product[a]	B Percentage of Employed[b]	Productivity Ratio		
			A/B	Agri- culture = 100	Industry = 100
Agriculture and livestock	19.7	50.0	0.39	100	26
Mining and petro-leum	6.1	1.0	6.00	1,538	408
Manufacturing	23.5	16.0	1.47	377	100
Construction	3.2	4.0	0.80	205	54
Other activities	47.5	29.0	1.63	418	110

[a]Derived from preliminary data in ECLA, *Economic Survey of Latin America 1960*, Part I, Table II-2.
[b]Estimate for 1960 based on 1950 data. (See Table 4.)

TABLE 8

GROWTH OF GROSS PRODUCT IN LATIN AMERICA, BY ACTIVITY, 1950-60

Activity	(1950 = 100)			Annual Rate of Growth		
	1955	1959	1960	1951-55	1956-60	1951-60
Gross domestic product	125	149	155	4.6	4.4	4.5
Agriculture	122	138	142	4.1	3.0	3.6
Manufacturing	130	178	197	5.4	8.7	7.0
Mining and petroleum	137	193	203	6.5	8.2	8.5
Construction	114	122	126	2.7	2.1	2.4
Trade and finance	128 ⎫			5.1		
Transport and com-munications	135 ⎪			6.2		
	⎬ 149	152 ⎬			3.9	4.3
Government services	120 ⎪			3.7		
Other services	120 ⎭			3.7		
Population	113	125	128	2.5	2.6	2.5
Per capita product	111	119	121	2.1	1.7	1.95

Source: ECLA, *Economic Bulletin for Latin America*, V, Statistical Supplement, Table 1. For 1960, preliminary estimates derived from ECLA, *Economic Survey of Latin America 1960*, Part I, Table II-2.

TABLE 9

LATIN AMERICA: AGRICULTURAL AND LIVESTOCK PRODUCTION, BY PRINCIPAL TYPES OF COMMODITIES, 1950-58

Commodity	1955 (1950 = 100)	1958 (1950 = 100)	Annual Rate of Growth 1951-55	Annual Rate of Growth 1956-58	Annual Rate of Growth 1951-58
Total agricultural and live-stock production	121	136[a]	3.9	3.0[b]	3.5[c]
Agricultural products	125	145[a]	4.6	3.8[b]	4.2[c]
Livestock products	106	115[a]	1.2	2.1[b]	1.6[c]
Grains	140	141	7.0	0.2	4.4
Roots and tubers	119	124	3.5	1.3	2.7
Dried leguminous products	123	127	4.2	1.0	3.0
Oilseeds	95	133	1.0	11.9	3.6
Sugar	105	139	1.0	9.7	4.2
Fruits	127	137	4.9	2.6	4.0
Nonalcoholic beverages	121	151	3.9	7.7	5.3
Fibers	130	139	5.4	2.3	4.2
Meat	106	125	1.2	4.8	2.8
Other	130	123	5.4	−1.8	2.6

Source: ECLA, *Economic Bulletin for Latin America*, V, No. 1 (March, 1960), Statistical Supplement, Table 5.

[a]1959.

[b]Growth rate for 1956-59.

[c]Growth rate for 1951-59.

TABLE 10

LATIN AMERICA: AGRICULTURAL AND LIVESTOCK PRODUCTION, BY PRINCIPAL COMMODITIES AND PRINCIPAL COUNTRIES, 1950-58

Commodity	1950	1955	1958	Percentage of 1958 Total	Annual Rate of Growth		
	(Thousands of Metric Tons)				1951-55	1956-58	1951-58
Wheat	7,864	11,884	9,753	100.0	8.6	-6.4	2.7
Argentina	5,144	7,690	5,810	59.6	8.4	-8.9	1.5
Chile	854	1,029	1,214	12.4	3.3	5.7	4.5
Mexico	587	850	1,150	11.8	7.7	10.6	8.8
Others	1,279	2,315	1,579	16.2	12.6	-12.0	2.7
Corn	12,961	17,053	20,760	100.0	5.7	6.8	6.1
Brazil	6,024	6,690	7,370	35.5	2.1	3.3	2.5
Mexico	3,122	4,490	5,150	24.8	7.2	4.7	6.5
Argentina	836	2,546	4,806	23.2	24.9	23.6	24.4
Others	2,979	3,327	3,434	16.5	2.2	1.1	1.8
Sugar	9,505	10,029	13,333	100.0	1.1	10.0	4.3
Cuba	5,558	4,528	5,779	43.3	-4.0	8.5	0.5
Brazil	1,403	2,073	3,004	22.5	8.2	13.2	10.0
Argentina	613	584	1,014	7.6	-0.9	20.2	6.5
Mexico	590	910	1,117	8.4	9.0	4.2	8.3
Others	1,341	1,934	2,419	18.1	7.6	7.7	7.6
Bananas[a]	303,708	388,436	410,204	100.0	5.0	1.8	3.8
Brazil	162,874	204,275	229,753	56.0	4.6	4.0	4.4
Ecuador	27,221	68,824	63,800	15.6	20.4	-2.4	11.2
Honduras	20,370	15,082	20,100	5.0	-5.8	10.1	-0.2
Costa Rica	15,744	18,205	16,700	4.0	3.0	-2.8	0.7
Others	77,499	82,050	79,851	19.4	1.1	-0.9	0.4

(continued)

Table 10 (continued)

Coffee	1,900	2,334	2,872	100.0	4.2	7.1	5.3
Brazil	1,071	1,370	1,696	59.0	5.0	7.4	5.9
Colombia	422	471	586	20.4	2.2	7.5	4.2
Mexico	66	86	120	4.2	5.4	11.8	8.1
Others	341	407	470	16.4	3.6	4.9	4.1
Cotton	912	1,281	1,353	100.0	7.0	1.8	5.1
Brazil	393	429	377	27.9	1.8	-4.2	-0.5
Mexico	260	508	529	39.1	14.3	1.4	9.3
Argentina	142	114	171	12.6	-4.3	14.5	2.4
Others	117	230	276	20.4	14.5	6.3	11.3
Rice	4,835	5,897	6,115	100.0	4.1	1.2	3.0
Brazil	3,218	3,738	3,829	62.6	3.1	0.8	2.2
Mexico	296	333	401	6.6	2.4	6.4	3.9
Colombia	219	320	390	6.4	7.9	6.8	7.5
Others	1,102	1,506	1,495	24.4	6.5	-0.2	3.9
Cacao	258	273	278	100.0	1.1	0.6	0.9
Brazil	153	158	164	59.0	0.6	1.2	0.9
Others	105	115	114	41.0	1.8	-0.3	1.0
Beef (slaughtered)[b]	23,682	24,161	29,325	100.0	0.4	6.7	2.7
Argentina	9,898	10,004	12,236	41.7	0.2	6.9	2.7
Brazil	5,965	6,031	7,857	26.8	0.2	9.2	3.5
Mexico	1,408	1,709	2,403	8.2	4.0	12.0	6.9
Others	6,411	6,417	6,829	23.3	0.1	2.1	0.8

Source: ECLA, *Economic Bulletin for Latin America*, V, No. 1 (March, 1960), Statistical Supplement, Table 4.
[a] Thousands of bunches.
[b] Thousands of head.

TABLE 11

LATIN AMERICA: MANUFACTURING OUTPUT, BY PRINCIPAL INDUSTRIES, 1950-59

Industrial Branches	1955 (1950 = 100)	1959 (1950 = 100)	Annual Rate of Growth 1951-55	Annual Rate of Growth 1956-59	Annual Rate of Growth 1951-59
Total	128	161	5.1	5.9	5.4
Food, drink and tobacco	125	146	4.6	4.0	4.3
Textiles	116	105	3.0	− 2.5	0.5
Paper and paper products	130	167	5.4	6.5	5.9
Chemicals, petroleum	154	231	9.0	10.7	9.7
Nonmetallic mineral products	145	169	7.7	3.9	6.0
Basic metals	133	169	5.9	6.2	6.0

Source: ECLA *Economic Bulletin for Latin America*, V (November, 1960), Statistical Supplement, Table 19.

TABLE 12

LATIN AMERICA: PRODUCTION OF SELECTED INDUSTRIAL COMMODITIES, 1950-60

| Commodity | 1950 | 1955 | 1960[a] | Annual Rate of Growth | | |
	(Thousands of Metric Tons)			1951-55	1956-60	1951-60
Cement	7,157	11,620	16,208	10.2	6.9	8.5
Pig iron	1,086	1,813	3,064	10.8	11.1	10.9
Steel ingots	1,377	2,534	4,576	13.0	12.6	12.8
Finished steel	1,366	2,591	4,392	13.4	11.1	12.4
Sulphuric acid	301	451	750[b]	8.4	18.5[c]	12.1[d]
Caustic soda	36	92	132[b]	20.6	12.8[c]	17.6[d]
Soda ash	12	62	81[b]	38.9	9.3[c]	27.0[d]
Wood pulp	281	377	797	6.1	16.2	11.0
Paper and board (except newsprint)	835	1,150	1,748	6.6	8.7	7.7
Newsprint	52	73	169	7.1	18.3	12.5
Automobiles and trucks (thousands of units)						
Domestic output[e]	...	11	170	...	172.9	...
Assemblage	...	54	69[f]	...	6.3[g]	...
Tractors[e] (units)	...	3,926	16,800	...	33.7	...
Railroad cars (units)	...	2,983	4,048[f]	...	7.9[g]	...

Source: ECLA, *Economic Bulletin for Latin America*, V, No. 1 (March, 1960), Statistical Supplement, Table 8; *Economic Survey of Latin America 1960*, Part II, Tables 1-6.

[a] Preliminary.
[b] 1958, estimated.
[c] Growth rate for 1956-58.
[d] Growth rate for 1951-58.
[e] Argentina and Brazil only.
[f] 1959.
[g] Growth rate for 1956-59.

TABLE 13

LATIN AMERICA: MINING OUTPUT, BY COMMODITIES, 1950-60

Commodity	1950	1955	1959	Percentage of 1959 Total
	(Thousands of Metric Tons)			
Crude petroleum	101,004	141,539	182,739	100.0
Venezuela	79,975	115,169	147,945	81.0
Mexico	10,363	12,793	13,956	7.6
Colombia	4,711	5,493	7,403	4.0
Argentina	3,357	4,365	6,357	3.5
Others	2,598	3,719	7,078	3.9
Index: 1950 = 100	100	140	181	
Iron ore	3,408	10,094	19,214	100.0
Venezuela	127	5,401	11,203	58.3
Brazil	1,351	2,300	3,500	18.2
Chile	1,771	940	2,476	12.9
Others	159	1,453	2,035	10.6
Index: 1950 = 100	100	296	564	
Coal	6,347	8,015	8,712	100.0
Colombia	1,010	1,800	2,400	27.5
Brazil	1,959	2,268	2,326	26.7
Chile	2,217	2,305	1,890	21.7
Mexico	912	1,342	1,586	18.1
Others	249	300	510	6.0
Index: 1950 = 100	100	126	137	
Sulphur	39	595	1,430	100.0
Mexico	11	521	1,388	97.0
Others	28	74	42	3.0
Index: 1950 = 100	100	1,526	3,666	
Copper	481	552	669	100.0
Chile	363	434	546	81.6
Mexico	62	55	57	8.5
Peru	30	43	49	7.3
Others	26	20	17	2.6
Index: 1950 = 100	100	115	139	

(continued)

Table 13 (continued)

Commodity	1950	1955	1959	Percentage of 1959 Total
	(Thousands of Metric Tons)			
Lead	335	376	360	100.0
Mexico	238	211	191	53.1
Peru	65	119	115	31.9
Others	52	46	54	15.0
Index: 1950 = 100	100	106	101	
Zinc	354	479	474	100.0
Mexico	234	249	264	55.7
Peru	88	166	157	33.1
Others	32	64	53	11.2
Index: 1950 = 100	100	135	134	
Tin (tons)	32,422	29,070	24,787	100.0
Bolivia	31,714	28,369	24,194	97.6
Others	708	701	593	2.4
Index: 1950 = 100	100	90	76	

Source: ECLA, *Economic Bulletin for Latin America*, V (November, 1960), Statistical Supplement), Table 20.

TABLE 14

SHARE OF LATIN AMERICA AND OTHER REGIONS
IN WORLD IMPORTS AND EXPORTS

Region	1876-1880	1896-1900	1913	1928	1937	1953[a]
			(Percentages)			
A. Exports						
Latin America	} 24.1	} 21.7	8.3	9.8	10.2	11.3
Asia, Africa, and Oceania			18.0	22.4	25.7	22.4
U. S. and Canada	11.7	14.5	14.8	19.8	17.1	27.4
United Kingdom	16.3	14.2	13.1	11.5	10.6	10.5
Northwest Europe	31.9	34.4	33.4	25.1	25.8	24.4
Other Europe	16.0	15.2	12.4	11.4	10.6	4.0
Total	100.0	100.0	100.0	100.0	100.0	100.0
B. Imports						
Latin America	} 26.3	} 23.0	7.0	7.6	7.2	10.0
Asia, Africa, and Oceania			16.4	21.0	23.1	23.6
U. S. and Canada	7.4	8.9	11.5	15.2	13.9	21.3
United Kingdom	22.5	20.5	15.2	15.8	17.8	13.6
Northwest Europe	31.9	36.5	36.5	27.9	27.8	} 31.5
Other Europe	11.9	11.0	13.4	12.5	10.2	
Total	100.0	100.0	100.0	100.0	100.0	100.0

Source: P. Lamartine Yates, *Forty Years of Foreign Trade* (London, George Allen and Unwin, 1959), Tables 6 and 7.
[a]Excluding centrally planned economies.

TABLE 15

SHARE OF LATIN AMERICA AND OTHER REGIONS
IN WORLD EXPORTS AND IMPORTS OF PRIMARY PRODUCTS

Region	1876-1880	1896-1900	1913	1928	1937	1953[a]
			(Percentages)			
A. Exports						
Latin America			12.6	15.8	16.1	19.8
	38.0	31.7				
Asia, Africa, and Oceania			24.0	28.9	34.0	34.0
U. S. and Canada	16.1	18.7	17.3	20.0	15.5	19.2
United Kingdom	3.1	3.9	6.2	4.8	4.8	4.8
Northwest Europe	22.6	27.6	25.2	14.5	15.6	18.2
Other Europe	20.2	18.1	14.7	16.0	13.7	4.0
Total	100.0	100.0	100.0	100.0	100.0	100.0
B. Imports						
Latin America			11.9	13.5	12.9	14.7
	51.8	47.5				
Asia, Africa, and Oceania			28.0	31.4	36.9	33.5
U. S. and Canada	7.7	9.6	12.1	12.8	10.6	19.1
United Kingdom	9.1	10.4	8.2	9.1	8.8	5.3
Northwest Europe	18.1	20.3	24.4	17.5	17.5	27.4
Other Europe	13.3	12.2	15.4	15.7	13.3	
Total	100.0	100.0	100.0	100.0	100.0	100.0

Source: Yates, *op. cit.*, Tables 19 and 21.
[a]Excluding centrally planned economies.

TABLE 16

SHARE OF AGRICULTURAL PRODUCTS IN WORLD TRADE, 1913-53

Commodity	Share of Latin America in Exports		Share of United States and Canada in Imports	
	1913	1953	1913	1953
	(Percentages)			
Food	21.1	24.6	9.7	22.2
Cereals	17.9	10.8	1.2	5.0
Livestock products	11.5	8.0	3.9	15.0
Beverages (tea, coffee, cacao)	62.1	63.8	30.2	52.5
Oilseeds and fats	11.4	6.3	6.6	13.3
Fruit and vegetables	14.2	12.7	18.4	21.3
Sugar	37.6	51.1	28.2	35.8
Agricultural materials	10.0	12.5	16.0	20.9
Fibers	6.3	17.7	10.8	13.5
Wood and wood pulp	2.9	4.2	9.9	27.4
Rubber and skins	25.1	7.8	34.6	35.5

Source: Yates, *op. cit.*, Tables 35, 36, 58, and 59.

TABLE 17
SHARE OF LATIN AMERICAN AND OTHER COUNTRIES IN VOLUME OF WORLD EXPORTS OF SELECTED AGRICULTURAL AND LIVE-STOCK COMMODITIES, 1909-13 AND 1953-54

Commodity	Thousands of Metric Tons		Percentage of Total	
	1909-13	1953-54	1909-13	1953-54
Food				
Wheat and flour	18,290	24,570	100.0	100.0
Argentina	2,590	2,800	14.2	11.4
Canada	2,460	8,080	13.5	32.9
United States	2,740	6,910	15.0	28.1
Australia	1,350	2,350	7.4	9.6
Others	9,150	4,430	49.9	18.0
Corn	6,480	5,375	100.0	100.0
Argentina	2,940	1,633	45.4	30.4
United States	1,100	2,641	17.0	49.1
Others	2,440	1,101	37.6	20.5
Meat	1,200	1,995	100.0	100.0
Argentina	338	273	32.3	13.7
Uruguay	72	72	6.0	3.6
New Zealand	124	370	10.3	18.5
Australia	146	302	12.2	15.1
Denmark	134	377	11.2	18.9
Others	336	601	28.0	30.2
Coffee	1,254	1,950	100.0	100.0
Brazil	759	794	60.5	40.7
Colombia	46	376	3.7	19.3
Mexico	22	71	1.8	3.6
Other Latin American countries	167	225	13.3	11.6
Others	160	484	20.7	24.8
Cacao	245	737	100.0	100.0
Brazil	32	115	13.1	15.6
Other Latin American countries[a]	171	173	69.9	23.5
Nigeria	3	103	1.2	14.0
Ghana	35	229	14.2	31.1
Others	4	117	1.6	15.8
Oilseeds and vegetable oils	2,720	3,934	100.0	100.0
Argentina	229	140	8.4	3.6
United States	133	457	4.9	11.6
Nigeria	162	568	6.0	14.4
Philippines	82	503	3.0	12.8
Indonesia	159	367	5.8	9.3
Others	1,955	1,899	71.9	48.3

(continued)

Table 17 (continued)

Commodity	Thousands of Metric Tons		Percentage of Total	
	1909-13	1953-54	1909-13	1953-54
Bananas	1,275	2,745	100.0	100.0
Ecuador	2	405	0.2	14.8
Colombia	107	196	8.4	7.1
Brazil	54	209	4.2	7.6
Central America[b]	400	935	31.4	34.1
Others	712	1,000	55.8	36.4
Sugar	7,080	12,825	100.0	100.0
Cuba	1,833	4,770	25.9	37.2
Dominican Republic	90	520	1.3	4.1
Peru	133	416	1.9	3.2
Philippines	258	854	3.6	6.7
British West Indies	203	682	2.9	5.3
Taiwan	157	698	2.2	5.4
Australia	15	700	0.2	5.5
Others	4,391	4,185	62.0	32.6
Agricultural materials				
Cotton	2,950	2,565	100.0	100.0
Mexico	—	245	—	9.6
Brazil	18	224	0.6	8.7
Peru	19	86	0.6	3.4
United States	2,002	792	67.9	30.9
Egypt	313	317	10.6	12.4
India	426	197	14.5	7.7
Others	172	704	5.8	27.3
Wool	1,083	1,135	100.0	100.0
Argentina	145	125	13.4	11.0
Uruguay	63	67	5.8	5.9
Australia	283	470	26.1	41.4
New Zealand	85	152	7.8	13.4
Others	507	321	46.9	28.3

Source: Yates, *op. cil.*, Tables 38, 40, 42, 48, 50, 52, 55, 56, 61, and 62.
[a]Including nonautonomous territories.
[b]Costa Rica, Guatemala, Honduras, Panama.

TABLE 18

WORLD EXPORTS OF SELECTED ORES AND METALS, AND
FUELS; QUANTUM AND PRICE INDICES, 1913, 1937, AND 1953

Commodity	Quantum Indices		Price Indices	
	1937	1953[a]	1937	1953[a]
		(1913 = 100)		
Ores and concentrates	222	281	129	235
Iron	300	187	141	281
Copper	105	177	87	190
Zinc	153	216	117	195
Lead	117	208	143	309
Tin	269	322	123	216
Others	159	610	111	200
Base metals	137	144	123	274
Iron	96	109	168	392
Copper	156	155	87	188
Zinc	98	135	117	196
Lead	205	194	139	309
Tin	134	111	123	217
Others	291	422	114	199
Fuels				
Coal and coke	94	69	123	293
Crude petroleum	835	10,060 ⎫	118	250
Refined petroleum	285	276 ⎭		

Source: Yates, *op. cit.*, Tables 72, 73, and 97.
[a]Excluding centrally planned economies.

TABLE 19

IRON ORE AND COPPER: EXPORTS OF PRINCIPAL
LATIN AMERICAN AND OTHER COUNTRIES, 1909-13 AND 1953-54

Country or Region	1909-13	1953-54	Percentage of Total 1909-13	1953-54
Iron ore	32.0	54.0	100.0	100.0
(millions of long tons)				
Cuba	1.6	—	5.0	—
Brazil	—	1.6	—	3.0
Chile	—	2.0	—	3.7
Venezuela	—	3.9	—	7.2
France	9.9	10.4	30.9	19.3
Spain	8.7	1.3	27.1	2.4
Sweden	6.3	14.1	19.7	26.1
French North Africa	1.9	5.3	6.0	9.8
Canada	1.4	5.0	4.4	9.3
United States	1.0	3.7	3.1	6.9
Others	1.2	6.7	3.8	12.3
	1913	**1953**	**1913**	**1953**
Copper concentrates	22	74	100.0	100.0
(millions of dollars)				
United States and				
Canada	3	28	13.6	37.8
Europe	4	20	18.2	27.0
Latin America	9	25	40.9	33.8
Other regions	6	1	27.3	1.4
Copper metal	304	889	100.0	100.0
(millions of dollars)				
United States and				
Canada	148	112	48.7	12.6
Europe	98	66	32.2	7.4
Latin America	30	295	9.9	33.2
Other regions	28	416	9.2	46.8

Source: Yates, *op. cit.*, Tables 75 and 79.

TABLE 20

EXPORTS OF ORES AND METALS BY PRINCIPAL LATIN
AMERICAN AND OTHER COUNTRIES, 1913 AND 1953-54

Country	1913	1953-54	Ratio 1953-54/1913
			(Thousands of Long Tons)
Copper ores and concentrates			
Chile	32	30	93.7
Peru	26	10	38.4
Mexico	79	40	50.6
Canada	...	43	...
Philippines	...	65	...
Copper metal			
Mexico	43	46[a]	106.9
Chile	...	328	...
United States	365	201	55.1
Canada	15	148	98.7
Rhodesia	7	378	540.0
Belgian Congo	...	221	...
Lead ores and concentrates			
Bolivia	2	20	100.0
Peru	...	46	...
Canada	...	54	...
Australia	153	42	27.5
South Africa	...	60	...
Lead metal			
Mexico	...	202	...
Peru	...	58	...
Canada	...	98	...
Australia	103	204	198.1
Spain	200	23	11.5
Zinc ores and concentrates			
Mexico	16	299	186.9
Peru	...	91	...
Bolivia	...	23	...
Australia	228	137	60.1
Algeria	80	33	41.3
Sweden	46	94	204.3
Canada	...	167	...

(continued)

Table 20 (continued)

Country	1913	1953-54	Ratio 1953-54/1913
		(Thousands of Long Tons)	
Zinc metal			
Mexico	...	48	...
Canada	...	167	...
United States	7	35	500.0
Belgium	122	142	116.4
Germany	126	73	57.9
Tin ores and concentrates			
Bolivia	44	32	72.7
Nigeria	4	11	275.0
Congo	...	18	...
Indonesia	2	46	230.0

Source: Yates, *op. cit.*, Tables 80, 83, 87, 90.
[a]Derived from *Anuario estadístico del comercio exterior* (México, 1954)

TABLE 21

EXPORTS OF CRUDE AND REFINED PETROLEUM: LATIN AMERICA AND OTHER REGIONS, 1929 AND 1955

	Millions of Long Tons		Percentage of Total		Ratio 1955/1929
	1929	1955	1929	1953-54	
Crude petroleum	35	235	100.0	100.0	671.4
Latin America	27	93	77.1	39.6	344.4
United States and Canada	4	3	11.4	1.3	75.0
Europe	–	–	–	–	–
Middle East	} 4	127 }	11.4	54.0 }	3,475.0
Other regions		12		5.1	
Refined petroleum	41	148	100.0	100.0	361.0
Latin America	14	65	34.1	43.9	464.3
United States and Canada	20	13	48.8	8.8	65.0
Europe	–	37	–	25.0	–
Middle East	} 7	16 }	17.1	10.8 }	471.4
Other regions		17		11.5	

Source: Yates, *op. cit.*, Table 100.

TABLE 22

QUANTUM AND PRICE INDICES OF EXPORTS
OF PRIMARY PRODUCTS AND MANUFACTURES

(1913 = 100)

Year	Quantum		Price	
	Primary Products	Manufactures	Primary Products	Manufactures
1876-1880	31	32	105	98
1896-1900	60	48	78	91
1913	100	100	100	100
1928	124	115	132	148
1937	136	108	100	122
1938	124	100	91	121
1948[a]	112	111	243	267
1953[a]	158	174	236	275

Source: Yates, *op. cit.*, derived from Tables 11 and 13.
[a]Excluding centrally planned economies.

TABLE 23

LATIN AMERICA: INDICES OF UNIT VALUE
OF EXPORTS AND IMPORTS, AND OF TERMS OF TRADE, 1950-59

(1950 = 100)

Year	Unit Value of Exports	Unit Value of Imports	Terms of Trade[a]
1950	100	100	100
1951	123	118	100
1952	111	122	91
1953	108	114	97
1954	114	115	102
1955	108	118	94
1956	105	119	92
1957	105	119	92
1958	98	118	87
1959	91	...	...

Source: ECLA, *Economic Bulletin for Latin America*, V (November, 1960),
Statistical Supplement, derived from Tables 26 and 28.
[a]Weighted index of the ratio of export over import prices of each country.

TABLE 24

LATIN AMERICAN EXPORTS, BY GROUPS OF COMMODITIES AND REGIONS OF DESTINATION, 1953

Commodity	Exports (Millions of Dollars)	Percentage Distribution by Destination[b]				Percentage of Each Group of Products and Each Destination in Total Exports[c]			
		U.S. and Canada	Europe	Japan	Non-industrial Countries	U.S. and Canada	Europe	Japan	Non-industrial Countries
Total[a]	7,620	50.4	24.9	2.8	21.9				
Food	3,796	57.1	28.1	1.6	13.2	28.5	14.0	0.8	6.6
Agricultural materials	1,209	27.4	45.3	11.6	15.7	4.3	7.2	1.8	2.5
Minerals and metals	2,226	50.8	8.8	0.4	40.0	14.8	2.6	0.1	11.7
Petroleum	1,477	39.6	6.8	0.1	53.5	7.7	1.3	—	10.4
Ores	348	73.3	19.0	2.0	5.7	3.3	0.9	0.1	0.3
Base metals	401	72.8	7.2	...	20.0	3.8	0.4	...	1.0
Manufactures	199	52.8	16.6	0.5	30.1	1.4	0.4	—	0.8
Other	190	55.8	26.3	3.2	14.7	1.4	0.7	0.1	0.4

Source: Yates, *op. cit.*, derived from Table 124.
[a]Total not comparable to that in Table 25.
[b]Percentage shares calculated on total exports of each commodity group.
[c]Percentage shares calculated in relation to total exports of $7,620 million.

TABLE 25

LATIN AMERICAN EXPORTS BY GROUPS OF PRODUCTS, 1913 AND 1953

Commodity	Millions of Dollars at Current Prices[a]		Percentage of Total	
	1913	1953	1913	1953
Food	1,019	3,999	64.5	48.2
Cereals	244	385	15.4	4.6
Livestock products	110	236	7.0	2.8
Beverages	327	2,111	20.7	25.5
Fats and oils	78	98	4.9	1.2
Fruit and vegetables	54	201	3.4	2.4
Sugar	144	725	9.1	8.7
Others	62	243	3.9	2.9
Agricultural materials	322	1,064	20.4	12.8
Fibers	118	796	7.5	9.6
Lumber and pulp	12	85	0.8	1.0
Hides and skins	92	95	5.8	1.1
Rubber	71	3	4.5	--
Others	29	85	1.8	1.0
Minerals and metals	204	3,098	12.9	37.4
Petroleum	5	2,304	0.3	27.8
Ores	121	102	10.5	4.7
Base metals	78	692	2.1	4.8
Manufactures and miscellaneous	36	133	2.3	1.6
Total	1,581	8,294	100.0	100.0

Source: Yates, *op. cit.*, derived from Tables A-32 and 123.
[a]Includes exports of nonautonomous territories.

TABLE 26

DISTRIBUTION OF LATIN AMERICAN EXPORTS, BY LEADING PRODUCTS

(Percentages of Dollar Value at Current Prices)

Commodity	1950	1955	1958
Total	100.0	100.0	100.0
Petroleum and its products	19.5	25.8	27.3
Coffee	21.5	22.0	17.8
Sugar	9.7	6.6	9.0
Cotton	4.4	5.4	4.1
Copper	2.8	5.0	2.5
Iron ore	0.1	1.1	2.4
Meat	1.7	1.6	2.2
Cacao	1.9	1.8	1.8
Wheat	3.2	3.4	1.7
Wool	5.2	2.5	1.7
Lead	1.3	1.1	1.1
Corn	0.7	0.3	1.0
Hides	3.0	1.4	1.0
Tobacco	0.8	0.7	0.7
Tin	0.8	0.7	0.7
Nitrates	1.1	0.7	0.5
Zinc	0.5	0.5	0.3
Quebracho (Tanning)	0.5	0.4	0.3
Others	21.3	19.0	24.0

Source: ECLA, *Economic Bulletin for Latin America*, V (November, 1960), Statistical Supplement, Table 34.

TABLE 27

PROJECTION OF LATIN AMERICAN EXPORTS TO THE UNITED STATES, BY PRINCIPAL PRODUCTS

Commodity	Volume	Millions of Dollars 1957	Volume (1957 = 100) 1965	1970	Current Value (1957 = 100) 1965	1970	Average Rate of Growth of Volume 1958-65	1958-70	Average Rate of Growth of Current Value 1958-65	1958-70
1. Food		1,809			95.9	107.8			-0.5	0.4
Coffee[a]	2,324	1,206	130.2	147.2	83.4	94.7	3.4	3.0	-2.2	0.4
Cacao[a]	257	69	151.7	165.3	169.5	185.5	5.1	3.9	6.8	4.9
Bananas[b]	1,454	149	123.4	135.2	122.1	135.5	2.4	2.4	2.5	2.4
Sugar (refined)[c]	3,225	355	116.9	129.3	111.2	131.3	2.0	2.0	1.3	2.1
Sugar (molasses)[d]	195	30	176.9	189.7	116.6	126.6	7.4	5.1	1.9	1.8
2. Minerals		1,498			119.4	158.2			2.2	3.6
Iron ore[e]	19.2	153	143.2	167.2	188.9	265.3	4.6	4.0	8.3	7.8
Copper[c]	347	204	142.3	188.7	144.6	193.6	4.5	5.0	4.8	5.2
Lead ore[c]	93	22	129.0	166.6	131.8	168.1	3.3	4.0	3.5	4.1
Lead (metal)[c]	138	37	134.4	166.6	135.1	170.2	3.8	4.0	3.8	4.2
Crude petroleum[f]	221	583	97.2	108.5	102.9	123.8	-0.3	0.6	0.1	1.5
Fuel oil[f]	170	446	102.3	136.4	101.1	145.9	2.6	2.4	0.1	2.9
Zinc (concentrates)[c]	334	42	118.2	149.7	133.3	171.4	3.2	3.2	3.7	4.2
Zinc (metal)[c]	46	11	152.2	184.7	181.8	218.1	5.4	4.8	7.8	6.2
3. Others		694			129.6	158.5			3.3	3.6
4. Total		4,001			110.6	135.5			1.3	2.4

Source: Louis O. Delwart, *The Future of Latin American Exports to the United States: 1965 and 1970* (Washington, D.C., National Planning Association), derived from Tables 4, 6, and 8-16. [a]Millions of pounds. [b]Thousands of tons. [c]Thousands of short tons. [d]Millions of gallons. [e]Millions of long tons. [f]Millions of barrels.

TABLE 28

LATIN AMERICA: PROJECTION OF THE DEMAND FOR EXPORTS, BY PRINCIPAL PRODUCTS, 1975

	1954-56		Projection to 1975		Increase	
Commodity	Millions of Dollars	Percentage of Total	Millions of Dollars at 1954-56 Prices	Percentage of Total	Per-centage	Average Rate of Growth
Food	3,556	43.6	4,970	35.0	40	1.7
Wheat and flour	241	3.0	266	1.9	10	0.5
Corn and coarse crops	82	1.0	135	1.0	64	2.5
Sugar	578	7.1	729	5.1	26	1.2
Fruit and vegetables	229	2.8	315	2.2	38	1.6
Coffee	1,900	23.3	2,797	19.7	47	2.0
Cacao	160	1.9	244	1.7	53	2.1
Others[a]	366	4.5	484	3.4	32	1.4
Agricultural raw materials	1,071	13.1	1,528	10.8	43	1.8
Cotton	511	6.3	525	3.7	3	0.1
Wool	263	3.2	437	3.1	66	2.6
Oilseeds	57	0.7	113	0.8	98	3.5
Hides	99	1.2	121	0.9	22	1.0
Others[b]	141	1.7	332	2.3	135	4.4

Minerals and metals	781	9.6	2,799	19.7	258	6.6
Iron ore	105	1.3	910	6.4	767	11.4
Copper	425	5.2	1,232	8.7	190	5.5
Lead	88	1.1	244	1.7	177	5.2
Zinc	46	0.6	254	1.8	452	8.9
Tin	59	0.7	60	0.4	2	0.1
Fertilizers	58	0.7	99	0.7	71	2.7
Petroleum and its products	1,932	23.7	2,789	19.6	44	1.8
Unspecified products	817	10.0	2,114	14.9	159	4.9
Total	8,157	100.0	14,200	100.0	74	2.8

Source: ECLA, *The Latin American Common Market*, Part B, derived from Tables 3 and 4.
aIncludes tobacco, edible oils and fats, meat and livestock, dairy produce, fish and fish products, and rice.
bIncludes vegetable fibers, *quebracho*, wood, pulp and mechanical pulp, and rubber.

TABLE 29

WESTERN EUROPE: PROJECTION OF IMPORTS OF SELECTED PRODUCTS[a]

Commodity	Imports 1954-56[b] (Millions of Dollars)	Increase through 1975 Per-centage	Increase through 1975 Average Rate of Growth
Food			
Meat and livestock	550	55	2.2
Wheat	740	0	0.0
Fruit and vegetables	670	45	1.9
Sugar	360	30	1.3
Coffee	740	50	2.0
Cacao	320	65	2.5
Others	70	70	2.7
Agricultural raw materials			
Tobacco	400	50	2.0
Feed	210	20	0.9
Wool	1,140	50	2.0
Cotton	1,050	10	0.5
Hard fibers	70	30	1.3
Hides and skins	330	20	0.9
Minerals and metals			
Crude petroleum and its products	2,080	150	4.7
Iron ore	110	800	11.6
Copper	750	110	3.8
Lead	90	110	3.8
Zinc	40	200	5.6
Tin	30	25	1.1

Source: United Nations, *Economic Survey of Europe in 1957*, Chapter V, derived from Tables 4, 5, and 6.

[a]Projected on basis of average annual growth rate of 3.5 per cent in Western European net product. Countries included in Organization for European Economic Cooperation (except Switzerland).

[b]Imports valued F.O.B.

TABLE 30

WESTERN EUROPE: PROJECTION TO 1975 OF FOOD AND RAW MATERIALS IMPORTS, BY REGION OF ORIGIN[a]

Region of Origin	Imports in 1954-56		Projection to 1975			
	Millions of Dollars	Percentage of Total	Millions of Dollars at 1954-56 Prices	Per- centage of Total	Increases	
					Per- centage	Average Rate of Growth
United States and Canada	2.8	19.7	4.0	16.5	43	1.8
Eastern Europe	0.5	3.5	0.8	3.3	60	2.4
Latin America	2.1	14.8	3.2	13.2	52	2.1
Nonautonomous Territories of Western European countries	3.8	26.7	7.9	32.5	107	0.3
Sterling area countries	3.7	26.1	5.9	24.3	59	2.4
Others	1.3	9.2	2.5	10.3	92	3.3
Total	14.2	100.0	24.3	100.0	71	2.7

Source: United Nations, *Economic Survey of Europe in 1957*, Chapter V, derived from Table 7.
[a]Projection assumes net product will grow at an average annual rate of 3.5 per cent.

TABLE 31

UNITED STATES AND CANADA: RATIO OF RAW MATERIALS CONSUMPTION TO GROSS PRODUCT

	Average 1926-28	Average 1947-49	Average 1955-57	Projection 1980
		(Percentage)		
Canada				
Industrial materials	8.19	7.80	7.13	6.30
Id. except sawlogs and fuelwood	5.41	5.97	5.78	5.69
Mineral fuels	2.66	2.61	2.82	2.81
Non-fuel minerals	1.48	2.14	1.84	1.78
Forest products	4.05	3.05	2.47	1.72
Id. except sawlogs and fuelwood	1.27	1.22	1.12	1.10
United States				
Industrial materials	6.07	5.31	5.10	4.71
Id. except sawlogs and fuelwood	4.79	4.60	4.58	4.47
Mineral fuels	3.19	3.14	3.01	2.91
Non-fuel minerals	1.29	1.20	1.32	1.30
Forest products	1.59	0.97	0.77	0.50
Id. except sawlogs and fuelwood	0.31	0.26	0.25	0.26

Source: Wilbert G. Fritz, *The Future of Industrial Raw Materials in North America* (Washington, D.C., National Planning Association, Canadian-American Committee, 1960), Table 3.

TABLE 32

LATIN AMERICA: NET FOREIGN EXCHANGE FROM TOURISM, 1955-59

(Millions of Dollars)

	1953	1956	1957	1958	1959[a]
Latin America	363.2	396.3	383.3	437.4	541.2
Argentina	...	4.0	0.5	-6.4	-5.6
Bolivia	...	-0.7	-0.7	-0.6	-0.8
Brazil	-12.0	-34.0	-40.0	-26.0	-31.0
Chile	-0.4	-5.6	-8.9	-8.2	-7.5
Colombia	-9.8	-12.6	-17.5	-5.6	-5.2
Costa Rica	0.2	0.6	1.0	1.4	1.0
Cuba	-3.0	4.3	25.9	19.4	18.9
Dominican Republic	-2.6	2.3	-0.5	-1.4	-1.0
Ecuador	-0.7	-0.4	-0.5	-0.3	-1.1
El Salvador	-21.6	-19.4	-12.6	-8.9	-12.9
Guatemala	2.3	2.1	2.4	2.9	3.3
Haiti	19.2	19.4	22.8	21.4	26.6
Honduras	-0.4	-0.4	-1.2	-1.3	-0.9
Mexico[b]	422.3	480.0	526.8	522.2	612.2
Nicaragua	-2.2	-4.2	-4.2	-4.6	-5.0
Panama	25.1	26.5	26.7	18.4	17.6
Paraguay	-0.5	...	-0.9	-0.2	-0.9
Peru	-3.1	-3.2	-3.4	0.5	0.2
Uruguay	1.0	1.7	10.1	13.8	22.1
Venezuela[c]	-50.6	-64.1	-137.5	-99.1	-88.8

Source: International Monetary Fund, *Balance of Payments Yearbook*, Vol. XII, 1955-59; and Bank of Mexico.

[a]Preliminary

[b]Gross receipts from border visits and travel to interior, minus tourist expenditure by Mexicans abroad (border purchases by Mexicans are not here considered tourist expenditure).

[c]Gross expenditure abroad.

TABLE 33

LATIN AMERICA: COST OF LIVING, 1950, 1955, 1960, AND JULY, 1961

Countries	1950	1955	1960 (1950 = 100)	Percentage Increases		Average Rate of Growth 1951-60		Average 1960 to July, 1961[a]
				1951-55	1956-60		1959-60	
Argentina	100	227	1,151	127	407	27.7	27	15
Bolivia	100	1,111	9,258	1,011	733	57.3	12	6
Brazil	100	232	721	132	211	21.8	35	34
Chile	100	555	2,137	455	285	35.8	12	8
Colombia	100	123	192	23	56	6.7	4	10
Costa Rica	100	111	119	11	7	1.8	1	2
Dominican Republic	100	106	106	6	—	0.6	-4	-9
Ecuador	100	115	114	15	-1	1.3	2	5
El Salvador	100	128	129	28	1	2.6	-1	—
Guatemala	100	110	110	10	—	1.0	-1	1
Haiti	100[b]	98	93	-2	-5	-0.7	-6	3
Honduras	100	125	121	25	-4	1.9	-2	4
Mexico	100	154	204	54	32	7.4	-5	1
Nicaragua	...[b]	100	93	...	-7	...	-2	2
Panama	100[b]	98	98	-2	—	—	—	—
Paraguay	100	769	1,382	669	80	29.7[c]	11	27
Peru	100	141	212	41	50	7.8	9	4
Uruguay	100	169	468	69	177	16.7	39	24
Venezuela	100	106	120	6	13	1.9	4	-4

Source: ECLA, *Economic Bulletin for Latin America*, V, Statistical Supplement; International Monetary Fund, *International Financial Statistics*.

[a]In some cases, April, May, or June.   [b]1952.   [c]Rate of growth: 1953-60.

TABLE 34

LATIN AMERICA: WHOLESALE PRICES, 1950, 1955, 1960, AND JULY, 1961

Country	1950	1955	1960 (1950 = 100)	1951-55	1956-60	Average Rate of Growth 1951-60	1959-60	Average 1960 to July, 1961[a]
							Percentage Increase	
Brazil	100	222	602	122	171	19.7	31	31
Chile	100	555	2,237	455	303	36.4	6	—
Colombia	100	122	220	22	80	8.1	4	8
Costa Rica	100	94	96	−6	2	−0.4	2	6
Dominican Republic	100[b]	107	113	7	6	1.2	3	−2
Ecuador	100[d]	101	101	1	—	0.1[c]	−2	4
El Salvador	100[d]	104	89	4	−15	−1.1[e]	—	−2
Guatemala	100	106	106	6	—	0.6	−1	—
Mexico	100	156	187	56	20	6.5	5	1
Nicaragua	100	182	169[f]	82	−7	5.3	−2	2
Paraguay	100	769	1,776	669	131	33.3	13	15
Peru	100	149	264	49	77	10.2	18	—
Venezuela	100	103	106	3	3	0.6	—	−2

Source: Same as for Table 33.

[a] In some cases, March, May, or June.
[b] 1952.
[c] Rate of growth: 1953-60.
[d] 1953.
[e] Rate of growth: 1954-60.
[f] Estimated with cost of living index.

TABLE 35

LATIN AMERICA: UNITED STATES DIRECT PRIVATE INVESTMENT

Country	1929	1936	1943	1950	1957	1959	Percentage of 1959 Total
			(Millions of Dollars)				
Total	3,462	2,803	2,721	4,445	7,434	8,218	100.0
Argentina	332	348	380	356	333	361	4.4
Bolivia	62	18	13	11	16	31	0.4
Brazil	194	194	233	644	835	839	10.2
Chile	423	484	328	540	666	729	8.9
Colombia	124	108	117	193	396	399	4.9
Costa Rica	22	13	30	60	62	60	0.7
Cuba	919	666	526	642	849	955	11.6
Dominican Republic	69	41	71	106	88	87	1.1
Ecuador	12	5	11	14	42	51	0.6
El Salvador	29	17	15	18	30	31	0.4
Guatemala	70	50	87	106	106	131	1.6
Haiti	14	10	14	13	35	36	0.4
Honduras	72	36	37	62	108	110	1.3
Mexico	682	480	286	415	739	759	9.2
Nicaragua	13	5	4	9	16	18	0.2
Panama	29	27	110	58	201	328	4.0
Paraguay	12	5	9	6	6	13	0.2
Peru	124	96	71	145	383	427	5.2
Uruguay	28	14	6	55	57	44	0.5
Venezuela	233	186	373	993	2,465	2,808	34.2

Source: U. S. Department of Commerce, *U. S. Business Investments in Foreign Countries*, 1960, Table 4.

TABLE 36

UNITED STATES DIRECT PRIVATE INVESTMENT IN FOREIGN COUNTRIES, BY REGIONS AND BY ACTIVITY, 1929, 1950, 1957, AND 1959

| | 1929 | 1950 | 1957 | 1959 | Percentage of Total | | | |
		(Billions of Dollars)			1929	1950	1957	1959
Total	7.5	11.8	25.3	29.7	100.0	100.0	100.0	100.0
Canada	2.0	3.6	8.6	10.0	26.7	30.5	34.0	34.3
Latin America	3.5	4.4	7.4	8.2	46.7	37.3	29.2	27.6
Europe	1.4	1.7	4.2	5.3	18.7	14.4	16.6	17.8
Africa	0.1	0.3	0.7	0.8	1.3	2.5	2.8	2.7
Asia	0.4	1.0	2.0	2.2	5.3	8.5	8.0	7.4
Oceania	0.1	0.3	0.7	0.9	1.3	2.5	2.8	3.0
International shipping	—	0.4	1.0	1.3	—	3.4	4.0	4.4
European dependencies in Western Hemisphere	—	0.1	0.6	0.8	—	0.8	2.4	2.7
Activity					100.0	100.0	100.0	100.0
Petroleum	1.1	3.4	9.1	10.4	14.6	28.8	35.9	35.0
Mining	1.2	1.1	2.4	2.8	16.0	9.3	9.5	9.4
Manufacturing	1.8	3.8	8.0	9.9	24.0	32.2	31.6	33.3
Public utilities	1.6	1.4	2.1	2.4	21.3	11.9	8.3	8.1
Trade	0.4	0.8	1.7	2.0	5.3	6.8	6.7	6.7
Agriculture	0.9	0.6	0.7	0.6	12.0	5.1	2.8	2.0
Other	0.5	0.7	1.3	1.6	6.7	5.9	5.1	5.4

Source: U. S. Department of Commerce, *op. cit.*, Tables 4 and 5.

TABLE 37

LATIN AMERICA: UNITED STATES DIRECT PRIVATE INVESTMENT BY COUNTRY AND BY ACTIVITY, 1959

	Total	Petro-leum	Mining	Manu-factur-ing	Public Utili-ties	Trade	Other
			(Millions of Dollars)				
Total	8,218	2,963	1,258	1,405	1,101	641	850
Percentage of total	100	36	15	17	13	8	11
Argentina	361	a	a	158	a	16	13
Brazil	839	82	5	438	192	101	21
Chile	729	a	526	21	a	20	a
Colombia	399	225	a	77	28	39	a
Cuba	955	143	a	115	313	a	281
Dominican Republic	87	a	a	a	5	2	44
Guatemala	131	20	a	a	63	5	36
Honduras	110	a	a	a	22	1	69
Mexico	759	30	137	355	118	83	36
Panama	328	29	16	8	21	117	136
Peru	427	79	242	31	19	36	19
Venezuela	2,808	2,164	a	160	29	166	a
Other countries	284	76	2	33	54	11	86

Source: U. S. Department of Commerce, *op. cit.*, Table 1.
[a]Included in total.

TABLE 38

LATIN AMERICA: INCREASE IN U. S. DIRECT PRIVATE INVESTMENT, BY COUNTRY AND BY ACTIVITY, 1950-59

(Millions of Dollars)

	Increase 1950-59	Percentage Share in the Increase, by Countries	Increase 1950-59					
			Petroleum	Mining	Manufacturing	Public Utilities	Trade	Other[a]
Total	3,773		1,730	630	625	174	399	214
Percentage share in the increase, by activity		100.0	46.6	16.9	16.6	4.6	10.2	5.7
Argentina	5	0.1	b	b	-3	-77	-19	-3
Brazil	195	5.2	-30	5	153	54	28	-8
Chile	189	5.0	b	175	-8	b	-4	-3
Colombia	206	5.4	113	b	52	-1	30	-7
Cuba	313	8.3	123	b	61	42	-21	12
Dominican Republic	-19	-0.5	b	b	-9	-6	1	-37
Guatemala	25	0.7	16	b	b	-9	2	36
Honduras	48	1.3	b	b	b	13	1	69
Mexico	344	9.1	17	16	222	11	53	25
Panama	270	7.2	23	16	6	3	106	131
Peru	282	7.5	79	187	15	19	23	18
Venezuela	1,815	48.1	1,307	b	136	19	142	-20
Other countries	98	2.6	58	-7	-7	14	1	16

Source: U. S. Department of Commerce, *op. cit.*, Tables 1 and 3.
[a] Includes agriculture, finance, insurance, and others.
[b] Included in total.

TABLE 39

LATIN AMERICA: NET EARNINGS OF UNITED STATES DIRECT PRIVATE INVESTMENTS, BY COUNTRY AND BY ACTIVITY, 1957

(Millions of Dollars)

Country	Total	Percentage of Total by Countries	Agriculture	Petroleum	Mining	Manufacturing	Public Utilities	Trade	Other
Total	1,096	100.0	73	638	95	129	33	81	47
Percentage share of total, by activity			6.6	58.2	8.7	11.8	3.0	7.4	4.3
Argentina	29	2.7	a	a	a	15	a	2	3
Brazil	69	6.3	a	7	2	44	4	7	1
Chile	47	4.3	—	a	42	1	a	2	—
Colombia	20	1.8	a	4	a	8	1	3	2
Cuba	73	6.7	39	4	a	9	12	4	2
Dominican Republic	9	0.8	a	a	a	a	1	—	—
Guatemala	2	0.2	a	-4	a	a	2	—	a
Honduras	5	0.4	a	a	a	a	2	—	a
Mexico	54	4.9	—	2	10	32	—	8	1
Panama	54	4.9	a	3	1	1	2	26	7
Peru	34	3.1	a	9	12	3	2	3	a
Venezuela	679	61.9	a	605	a	14	5	23	15
Other countries	22	2.0	18	-2	1	1	4	3	2

Source: U. S. Department of Commerce, *op. cit.*, Table 38.

a Included in total.

— Less than $500,000.

TABLE 40

LATIN AMERICA: GROSS INVESTMENT RATIO, BY COUNTRIES, 1950-58

(Percentage of Gross National Product)[a]

Country	1950	1955	1957	1958
Latin America	16.5	16.9	18.4	17.4
Argentina	22.9	21.2	23.8	22.8
Bolivia	11.3	20.5	20.0	...
Brazil	13.3	13.4	12.8	13.1
Chile	8.9	10.9	9.9	8.3
Colombia	17.7	23.6	21.6	21.9
Costa Rica	17.9	24.5	25.3	24.9
Cuba	11.0	17.5	18.7	19.5
Dominican Republic	15.2	21.4	22.0	...
Ecuador	8.6	13.9	13.1	13.1
Guatemala	9.6	10.1	12.5	13.0
Mexico	13.7	13.7	15.5	14.8
Peru	15.7	20.6	21.3	20.8
Venezuela	23.0	20.2	27.1	21.8

Source: ECLA, *Economic Bulletin for Latin America*, IV, No. 2 (October, 1959), Statistical Supplement, Table 7.

[a]Calculated from values at 1950 prices.

TABLE 41

AVERAGE PERCENTAGE FLUCTUATIONS
IN SELECTED PRIMARY PRODUCTS, 1920-38 AND 1948-57

Commodity	Average 1920-38			Average 1948-57		
	Value	Unit Value	Volume	Value	Unit Value	Volume
Cacao	19	19	5	17	19	7
Coffee	16	15	5	9	11	7
Corn	18	14	17	15	13	10
Wheat	16	12	8	15	8	12
Rice	13	12	6	12	11	8
Beef	15	12	7	10	8	13
Mutton	11	9	6	14	7	10
Sugar	13	16	9	6	6	4
Bananas	8	10	8	4	2	4
Tobacco	12	9	5	6	4	6
Wool	19	21	8	17	17	10
Cotton	15	15	5	14	13	8
Tin	26	16	17	14	10	15
Lead	25	20	9	16	18	14
Copper	23	16	12	15	15	6
Zinc	23	15	13	17	18	9
Crude Petroleum	18	17	7	4	5	3

Source: United Nations, *World Economic Survey, 1958*, Chap. I, Table 13.

TABLE 42

ANNUAL PRICE CHANGE OF SELECTED PRIMARY PRODUCTS, 1951-60

(Percentage)

Commodity	1951/ 1950	1952/ 1951	1953/ 1952	1954/ 1953	1955/ 1954	1956/ 1955	1957/ 1956	1958/ 1957	1959/ 1958	1960/ 1959
Cotton	28.1	-16.9	-18.3	6.4	-3.9	-15.4	-5.8	-4.4	-11.3	0.8
Coffee	6.7	-0.3	8.0	34.0	-27.2	2.5	-1.9	-14.7	-22.5	-2.6
Sugar	14.1	-26.5	-18.2	-4.4	-0.7	7.1	49.7	-32.2	-15.1	...
Cacao	11.1	-0.6	4.9	55.5	-35.2	-27.5	12.2	43.4	-22.9	-14.9
Wool	45.8	-42.7	2.2	-3.1	-7.5	0.2	13.1	-25.8	13.1	4.6
Wheat	7.6	-0.4	-6.3	3.1	-2.2	-1.8	0.9	-9.4	-2.5	0.5
Beef	10.1	25.5	10.8	4.7	16.9	-22.0	8.0	14.0	4.5	-4.6
Bananas	1.3	-2.4	0.5	...	1.3	0.6	3.8	-1.9	-1.3	-5.7
Zinc	44.2	-14.2	-49.5	5.0	16.3	7.2	-15.5	-19.5	24.0	7.5
Lead	52.8	-17.6	-31.0	4.8	10.2	9.3	-18.3	-23.4	-3.3	1.5
Copper	23.2	18.5	-3.5	-0.7	42.1	-9.0	-33.3	-8.7	21.2	2.4
Tin	45.0	-10.7	-24.1	-1.7	2.9	6.5	-4.2	-2.6	6.9	1.4
Petroleum and its products	—	5.6	4.2	—	—	9.1	-3.7	-2.0	—	

Source: International Monetary Fund, *International Financial Statistics*, October, 1958, and October, 1961.
Cotton, zinc, beef, copper, lead, and tin: U.K. prices.
Wheat, bananas, coffee, petroleum and its products, cacao, and wool: U.S. prices.
Sugar: world market price for Cuban sugar.

Index